English for Specific Purposes

A learning-centred approach

*Tom Hutchinson and
Alan Waters*

Originally published in The New Directions
in Language Teaching Series, edited by
Howard B. Altman and Peter Strevens

CAMBRIDGE
UNIVERSITY PRESS

Published by the Press Syndicate of the University of Cambridge
The Pitt Building, Trumpington Street, Cambridge CB2 1RP
40 West 20th Street, New York, NY 10011–4211, USA
10 Stamford Road, Oakleigh, Melbourne 3166, Australia

First published 1987
Eleventh printing 1996

Printed in Great Britain at
Bell & Bain Ltd, Glasgow

Library of Congress catalogue card number: 86–9528

British Library cataloguing in publication data

Hutchinson, Tom, 1948–

English for Specific Purposes: a learning-centred approach.
1. English language – Study and teaching
– Foreign speakers
I. Title   II. Waters, Alan, 1947–
III. Series
428.2′4′07   PE1128.A2

ISBN 0 521 26732 3   hard covers
ISBN 0 521 31837 8   paperback

English for Specific Purposes
A learning-centred approach

CAMBRIDGE LANGUAGE TEACHING LIBRARY

A series covering central issues in language teaching and learning, by authors who have expert knowledge in their field.

In this series:

To Pam and Mary

Contents

Thanks

We would like to express our gratitude to all those who have, knowingly or otherwise, helped to shape the ideas that have gone into this book. First of all, we would like to thank our colleagues at the University of Lancaster, both in the Institute for English Language Education and in the Department of Linguistics, and all the students and teachers who have attended our courses there. We are also grateful to the staff and students of the many institutions and projects with whom we have been associated around the world. In particular, we would like to mention the Brazilian National ESP Project; King Mongkut's Institute of Technology, Thonburi, Thailand; the Sri Lankan Ministry of Higher Education ESP Project; Kuwait University Language Centre; De La Salle University, Manila, Philippines; the University of the Philippines; the French ESP Group; the Technical Education Advisers' Project, Indonesia; the Ministries of Education in Croatia and Slovenia, Yugoslavia. We would also like to express our gratitude to the British Council, whose support has made many of our contacts with these institutions and projects possible. Finally, we would like to acknowledge our debt to all those ESP practitioners around the world, without whom this book would have no purpose.

Tom Hutchinson & Alan Waters
Lancaster, 1986

Introduction

To travel hopefully is a better thing than to arrive, and the true success is to labour.

(Robert Louis Stevenson)

The City of ELT

Once upon a time there was a city called ELT. The people of ELT led a comfortable, if not extravagant, life, pursuing the noble goals of literature and grammar. There were differences, of course: some people preferred to call themselves EFL people, while others belonged to a group known as ESL. But the two groups lived in easy tolerance of each other, more united than disunited.

Now it happened that the city was surrounded by high mountains and legend had it that the land beyond the mountains was inhabited by illiterate and savage tribes called Scientists, Businessmen and Engineers. Few people from ELT had ever ventured into that land. Then things began to change. Some of the people in ELT became restless. The old city could not support its growing population and eventually some brave souls set off to seek their fortune in the land beyond the mountains. Many in ELT were shocked at the prospect. It was surely no place for people brought up in the gentle landscape of English literature and language.

But, as it turned out, the adventurers found a rich and fertile land. They were welcomed by the local inhabitants and they founded a new city, which they called ESP. The city flourished and prospered as more and more settlers came. Soon there were whole new settlements in this previously uncharted land. EST and EBE were quickly followed by EAP and EOP (the latter confusingly also known as EVP and VESL). Other smaller groups took on the names of the local tribes to found a host of new towns called English for Hotel Staff, English for Marine Engineers, English for Medical Science and so on. A future of limitless expansion and prosperity looked assured.

But as with all things the reality proved less rosy. A number of people at the frontiers were forced to abandon their settlements and return to the larger cities. Many settlers, who had come to the newly developed land because ELT could no longer provide them with a living, longed for the comforts and certainties of the old city. Others were confused as to where their loyalties lay: were they still citizens of ELT? Was EAP an independent city or a suburb of ESP? Did the people of English for Medical Science owe allegiance to EAP, EOP or ESP? Worst of all, there were even examples of groups from ELT being transported against their will to the new territories. Added to all this, the Scientists, Businessmen and other tribes were becoming more demanding. Some began to resent the interference of the settlers in their area; others complained that the promised benefits had not materialised. The future in short began to look, if not gloomy, then a little confused and uncertain for the brave new world of ESP.

I

Which brings us to this book. It will, we hope, serve as a guide to all present and future inhabitants of ESP, revealing both the challenges and pleasures to be enjoyed there and the pitfalls to be avoided. But first let us take a moment to explain the title we have given to the book, for in doing so, we will not only explain our reasons for writing it, but will also be able to present a plan of the itinerary we shall follow. What, then, is a learning-centred approach to ESP?

ESP, like any form of language teaching, is primarily concerned with learning. But it is our view that in its development up to now, ESP has paid scant attention to the question of *how* people learn, focussing instead on the question of *what* people learn. It has, in other words, been language-centred in its approach. We would not wish to dismiss this language-centred approach. It has provided some very important insights into the nature of specific language needs. However, we feel that, if it is to have any real and lasting value, ESP must be founded in the first instance on sound principles of learning, and it is with this purpose in view that we have proposed a learning-centred approach to ESP. In the following pages we shall explain what this shift in focus entails for the ESP practitioner.

The book is divided into four sections (see figure 1).

Section 1 is an overview of the origins and development of ESP and considers the question of how ESP fits into the general landscape of English Language Teaching.

Section 2 looks at basic principles and techniques in course design. How, in other words, do you create a course to fit the needs of a particular group of learners?

Section 3 is concerned with the practical applications of the course design in the form of a syllabus, materials, methodology and assessment. Put briefly, having completed your course design, what do you do with it?

Section 4 considers the role of the ESP teacher and provides information about resources to help the teacher.

The book is intended to be very much a practical guide, and to this end we have supplied a number of Tasks at the end of each chapter. These are to get you thinking about the issues that are raised in that section and, in particular, to help you relate our necessarily general points to your own specific situation. If you are concerned with teacher-training, these tasks may also be useful as workshop or seminar activities. Although they are placed at the end of the chapter, they can often be more valuable if done before reading the chapter itself.

Your guide, route and mode of travel presented, it remains only to wish you an interesting and enjoyable journey.

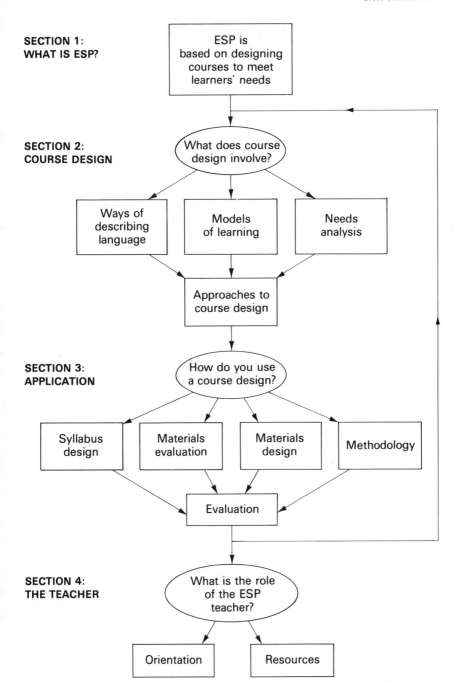

Figure 1: Outline of 'A learning-centred approach to ESP'

Section 1   *What is ESP?*

> Particulars are not to be examined till the whole has been surveyed.
>
> (Dr Samuel Johnson: *Preface to Shakespeare*)

Our concern in this section is to arrive at a workable definition of ESP. But rather than give a straight answer now to the question 'What is ESP?', we would prefer to let it gradually emerge as we work through the section. Let us begin instead with a simpler question: 'Why ESP?' After all, the English Language world got along well enough without it for many years, so why has ESP become such an important (some might say the most important) part of English language teaching? In the following three chapters we shall briefly survey the factors which led to the emergence of ESP in the late 1960s and the forces, both theoretical and practical, which have shaped its subsequent development. In Section 2 we shall look in greater detail at the elements we outline in this section.*

* It is our intention here only to establish the background for the concepts and procedures we wish to present in this book. For a thorough and detailed explanation of the development of ideas and practices in ESP, we would recommend *Episodes in ESP* by John Swales (Pergamon, 1985).

1 The origins of ESP

> We will now discuss in a little more detail the struggle for
> existence.
>
> (Charles Darwin: *The Origin of Species*)

As with most developments in human activity, ESP was not a planned
and coherent movement, but rather a phenomenon that grew out of a
number of converging trends. These trends have operated in a variety
of ways around the world, but we can identify three main reasons
common to the emergence of all ESP.

1 The demands of a Brave New World

The end of the Second World War in 1945 heralded an age of enormous
and unprecedented expansion in scientific, technical and economic
activity on an international scale. This expansion created a world unified
and dominated by two forces – technology and commerce – which in
their relentless progress soon generated a demand for an international
language. For various reasons, most notably the economic power of the
United States in the post-war world, this role fell to English.

The effect was to create a whole new mass of people wanting to learn
English, not for the pleasure or prestige of knowing the language, but
because English was the key to the international currencies of technology
and commerce. Previously the reasons for learning English (or any other
language) had not been well defined. A knowledge of a foreign language
had been generally regarded as a sign of a well-rounded education, but
few had really questioned why it was necessary. Learning a language
was, so to speak, its own justification. But as English became the
accepted international language of technology and commerce, it created
a new generation of learners who knew specifically why they were
learning a language – businessmen and -women who wanted to sell their
products, mechanics who had to read instruction manuals, doctors who
needed to keep up with developments in their field and a whole range of
students whose course of study included textbooks and journals only
available in English. All these and many others needed English and, most
importantly, they knew why they needed it.

This development was accelerated by the Oil Crises of the early 1970s, which resulted in a massive flow of funds and Western expertise into the oil-rich countries. English suddenly became big business and commercial pressures began to exert an influence. Time and money constraints created a need for cost-effective courses with clearly defined goals.

The general effect of all this development was to exert pressure on the language teaching profession to deliver the required goods. Whereas English had previously decided its own destiny, it now became subject to the wishes, needs and demands of people other than language teachers. English had become accountable to the scrutiny of the wider world and the traditional leisurely and purpose-free stroll through the landscape of the English language seemed no longer appropriate in the harsher realities of the market place.

2 A revolution in linguistics

At the same time as the demand was growing for English courses tailored to specific needs, influential new ideas began to emerge in the study of language. Traditionally the aim of linguistics had been to describe the rules of English usage, that is, the grammar. However the new studies shifted attention away from defining the formal features of language usage to discovering the ways in which language is actually used in real communication (Widdowson, 1978). One finding of this research was that the language we speak and write varies considerably, and in a number of different ways, from one context to another. In English language teaching this gave rise to the view that there are important differences between, say, the English of commerce and that of engineering. These ideas married up naturally with the development of English courses for specific groups of learners. The idea was simple: if language varies from one situation of use to another, it should be possible to determine the features of specific situations and then make these features the basis of the learners' course.

Swales (1985) presents an article by C. L. Barber on the nature of Scientific English which was published as early as 1962. But it was the late 1960s and early 1970s which saw the greatest expansion of research into the nature of particular varieties of English – for example, descriptions of written scientific and technical English by Ewer and Latorre (1969), Swales (1971), Selinker and Trimble (1976) and others. Most of the work at this time was in the area of English for Science and Technology (EST) and for a time ESP and EST were regarded as almost synonymous. But there were studies in other fields too, such as the

7

analysis of doctor-patient communication by Candlin, Bruton and Leather (1976).

In short, the view gained ground that the English needed by a particular group of learners could be identified by analysing the linguistic characteristics of their specialist area of work or study. 'Tell me what you need English for and I will tell you the English that you need' became the guiding principle of ESP.

3 Focus on the learner

New developments in educational psychology also contributed to the rise of ESP, by emphasising the central importance of the learners and their attitudes to learning (e.g. Rodgers, 1969). Learners were seen to have different needs and interests, which would have an important influence on their motivation to learn and therefore on the effectiveness of their learning. This lent support to the development of courses in which 'relevance' to the learners' needs and interests was paramount. The standard way of achieving this was to take texts from the learners' specialist area – texts about Biology for Biology students etc. The assumption underlying this approach was that the clear relevance of the English course to their needs would improve the learners' motivation and thereby make learning better and faster.

The growth of ESP, then, was brought about by a combination of three important factors: the expansion of demand for English to suit particular needs and developments in the fields of linguistics and educational psychology. All three factors seemed to point towards the need for increased specialisation in language learning.

Tasks

1 Why was ESP introduced in your country or teaching institution? What kinds of ESP are taught?

2 'Tell me what you need English for and I will tell you the English that you need' (p. 8). How justifiable do you think this claim is for ESP?

3 'The clear relevance of the English course to their needs would improve the learners' motivation and thereby make learning better and faster' (p. 8).
   a) Give three ways in which 'relevance' can be achieved.
   b) In what ways can motivation affect language learning?

2 The development of ESP

The best laid schemes o' mice and men
Gang aft a-gley.

(Robert Burns)

From its early beginnings in the 1960s ESP has undergone three main phases of development. It is now in a fourth phase with a fifth phase starting to emerge. We shall describe each of the five phases in greater detail in later chapters, but it will provide a useful perspective to give a brief summary here. It should be pointed out first of all that ESP is not a monolithic universal phenomenon. ESP has developed at different speeds in different countries, and examples of all the approaches we shall describe can be found operating somewhere in the world at the present time. Our summary must, therefore, be very general in its focus.

It will be noticeable in the following overview that one area of activity has been particularly important in the development of ESP. This is the area usually known as EST (English for Science and Technology). Swales (1985) in fact uses the development of EST to illustrate the development of ESP in general:

'With one or two exceptions... English for Science and Technology has always set and continues to set the trend in theoretical discussion, in ways of analysing language, and in the variety of actual teaching materials.'

We have not restricted our own illustrations to EST in this book, but we still need to acknowledge, as Swales does, the pre-eminent position of EST in the ESP story.

1 The concept of special language: register analysis

This stage took place mainly in the 1960s and early 1970s and was associated in particular with the work of Peter Strevens (Halliday, McIntosh and Strevens, 1964), Jack Ewer (Ewer and Latorre, 1969) and John Swales (1971). Operating on the basic principle that the English of, say, Electrical Engineering constituted a specific register different from that of, say, Biology or of General English, the aim of the analysis

9

was to identify the grammatical and lexical features of these registers. Teaching materials then took these linguistic features as their syllabus. A good example of such a syllabus is that of *A Course in Basic Scientific English* by Ewer and Latorre (1969) (see below p. 26).

In fact, as Ewer and Latorre's syllabus shows, register analysis revealed that there was very little that was distinctive in the sentence grammar of Scientific English beyond a tendency to favour particular forms such as the present simple tense, the passive voice and nominal compounds. It did not, for example, reveal any forms that were not found in General English. But we must be wary of making unfair criticism. Although there was an academic interest in the nature of registers of English *per se*, the main motive behind register analyses such as Ewer and Latorre's was the pedagogic one of making the ESP course more relevant to learners' needs. The aim was to produce a syllabus which gave high priority to the language forms students would meet in their Science studies and in turn would give low priority to forms they would not meet. Ewer and Hughes-Davies (1971), for example, compared the language of the texts their Science students had to read with the language of some widely used school textbooks. They found that the school textbooks neglected some of the language forms commonly found in Science texts, for example, compound nouns, passives, conditionals, anomalous finites (i.e. modal verbs). Their conclusion was that the ESP course should, therefore, give precedence to these forms.

2 Beyond the sentence: rhetorical or discourse analysis

There were, as we shall see, serious flaws in the register analysis-based syllabus, but, as it happened, register analysis as a research procedure was rapidly overtaken by developments in the world of linguistics. Whereas in the first stage of its development, ESP had focussed on language at the sentence level, the second phase of development shifted attention to the level above the sentence, as ESP became closely involved with the emerging field of discourse or rhetorical analysis. The leading lights in this movement were Henry Widdowson in Britain and the so-called Washington School of Larry Selinker, Louis Trimble, John Lackstrom and Mary Todd-Trimble in the United States.

The basic hypothesis of this stage is succinctly expressed by Allen and Widdowson (1974):

'We take the view that the difficulties which the students encounter arise not so much from a defective knowledge of the system of English, but from an unfamiliarity with English use, and that consequently their needs cannot be met by a course which simply provides further practice in the composition of sentences, but only by one which develops a knowledge of how sentences are used in the performance of different communicative acts.'

Register analysis had focussed on sentence grammar, but now attention shifted to understanding how sentences were combined in discourse to produce meaning. The concern of research, therefore, was to identify the organisational patterns in texts and to specify the linguistic means by which these patterns are signalled. These patterns would then form the syllabus of the ESP course. The Rhetorical Process Chart below (from *EST: A Discourse Approach* by Louis Trimble (1985)) is representative of this approach:

Level	Description of level
A.	The objectives of the total discourse EXAMPLES: 1. Detailing an experiment 2. Making a recommendation 3. Presenting new hypotheses or theory 4. Presenting other types of EST information
B.	The general rhetorical functions that develop the objectives of Level A EXAMPLES: 1. Stating purpose 2. Reporting past research 3. Stating the problem 4. Presenting information on apparatus used in an experiment – a) Description b) Operation 5. Presenting information on experimental procedures
C.	The specific rhetorical functions that develop the general rhetorical functions of Level B EXAMPLES: 1. Description: physical, function, and process 2. Definition 3. Classification 4. Instructions 5. Visual–verbal relationships
D.	The rhetorical techniques that provide relationships within and between the rhetorical units of Level C EXAMPLES: I. Orders 1. Time order 2. Space order 3. Causality and result II. Patterns 1. Causality and result 2. Order of importance 3. Comparison and contrast 4. Analogy 5. Exemplification 6. Illustration

Figure 2: Rhetorical Process Chart

As in stage 1 there was a more or less tacit assumption in this approach that the rhetorical patterns of text organisation differed significantly between specialist areas of use: the rhetorical structure of science texts was regarded as different from that of commercial texts, for example. However, this point was never very clearly examined (see Swales, 1985, pp. 70–1) and indeed paradoxically, the results of the research into the discourse of subject-specific academic texts were also used to make observations about discourse in general (Widdowson, 1978).

The typical teaching materials based on the discourse approach taught students to recognise textual patterns and discourse markers mainly by means of text-diagramming exercises (see below p. 36). The *English in Focus* series (OUP) is a good example of this approach.

3 Target situation analysis

The stage that we come to consider now did not really add anything new to the range of knowledge about ESP. What it aimed to do was to take the existing knowledge and set it on a more scientific basis, by establishing procedures for relating language analysis more closely to learners' reasons for learning. Given that the purpose of an ESP course is to enable learners to function adequately in a target situation, that is, the situation in which the learners will use the language they are learning, then the ESP course design process should proceed by first identifying the target situation and then carrying out a rigorous analysis of the linguistic features of that situation. The identified features will form the syllabus of the ESP course. This process is usually known as *needs analysis*. However, we prefer to take Chambers' (1980) term of 'target situation analysis', since it is a more accurate description of the process concerned.

The most thorough explanation of target situation analysis is the system set out by John Munby in *Communicative Syllabus Design* (1978). The Munby model produces a detailed profile of the learners' needs in terms of communication purposes, communicative setting, the means of communication, language skills, functions, structures etc. (see below p. 55).

The target situation analysis stage marked a certain 'coming of age' for ESP. What had previously been done very much in a piecemeal way, was now systematised and learner need was apparently placed at the centre of the course design process. It proved in the event to be a false dawn. As we shall see in the following chapters, the concept of needs that it was based on was far too simple.

4 Skills and strategies

We noted that in the first two stages of the development of ESP all the analysis had been of the surface forms of the language (whether at sentence level, as in register analysis, or above, as in discourse analysis). The target situation analysis approach did not really change this, because in its analysis of learner need it still looked mainly at the surface linguistic features of the target situation.

The fourth stage of ESP has seen an attempt to look below the surface and to consider not the language itself but the thinking processes that underlie language use. There is no dominant figure in this movement, although we might mention the work of Françoise Grellet (1981), Christine Nuttall (1982) and Charles Alderson and Sandy Urquhart (1984) as having made significant contributions to work on reading skills. Most of the work in the area of skills and strategies, however, has been done close to the ground in schemes such as the National ESP Project in Brazil (see below p. 172) and the University of Malaya ESP Project (see ELT Documents 107 and *Skills for Learning* published by Nelson and the University of Malaya Press).

Both these projects were set up to cope with study situations where the medium of instruction is the mother tongue but students need to read a number of specialist texts which are available only in English. The projects have, therefore, concentrated their efforts on reading strategies.*

The principal idea behind the skills-centred approach is that underlying all language use there are common reasoning and interpreting processes, which, regardless of the surface forms, enable us to extract meaning from discourse. There is, therefore, no need to focus closely on the surface forms of the language. The focus should rather be on the underlying interpretive strategies, which enable the learner to cope with the surface forms, for example guessing the meaning of words from context, using visual layout to determine the type of text, exploiting cognates (i.e. words which are similar in the mother tongue and the target language) etc. A focus on specific subject registers is unnecessary in this approach, because the underlying processes are not specific to any subject register.

'It was argued that reading skills are not language-specific but universal and that there is a core of language (for example, certain structures of argument and forms of presentation) which can be identified as "academic" and which is not subject-specific.' (Chitravelu, 1980)

---

* It is interesting to note, however, that not all such projects have such a focus. The ESP project at King Mongkut's Institute of Technology in Bangkok, Thailand, for example, has to cope with a very similar study situation, but the focus here is on the full range of skills (reading, writing, listening, speaking).

As has been noted, in terms of materials this approach generally puts the emphasis on reading or listening strategies. The characteristic exercises get the learners to reflect on and analyse how meaning is produced in and retrieved from written or spoken discourse. Taking their cue from cognitive learning theories (see below p. 43), the language learners are treated as thinking beings who can be asked to observe and verbalise the interpretive processes they employ in language use.

5 A learning-centred approach

In outlining the origins of ESP (pp. 6–8), we identified three forces, which we might characterise as need, new ideas about language and new ideas about learning. It should have become clear that in its subsequent development, however, scant attention has been paid to the last of these forces – learning. All of the stages outlined so far have been fundamentally flawed, in that they are all based on descriptions of language *use*. Whether this description is of surface forms, as in the case of register analysis, or of underlying processes, as in the skills and strategies approach, the concern in each case is with describing what people *do* with language. But our concern in ESP is not with language *use* – although this will help to define the course objectives. Our concern is with language *learning*. We cannot simply assume that describing and exemplifying what people do with language will enable someone to learn it. If that were so, we would need to do no more than read a grammar book and a dictionary in order to learn a language. A truly valid approach to ESP must be based on an understanding of the processes of language *learning*.

This brings us to the fifth stage of ESP development – the learning-centred approach, which will form the subject of this book. The importance and the implications of the distinction that we have made between language *use* and language *learning* will hopefully become clear as we proceed through the following chapters.

Tasks

1 Which of the stages outlined above has your country experienced? Has it developed in a completely different way?

2 Why do you think EST has set the trends in the development of ESP?

3 How far would you agree with Widdowson and Allen's assertion (pp. 10–11)?

4 An information leaflet about the Brazilian ESP Project summarises its aims as follows:

'The "specific purpose" most common within the participant universities is the reading of specialist literature in English. Consequently there is a consensus within the project to focus on the teaching of reading strategies with the use of authentic materials and the use of the native language in spoken classroom discourse. The teaching of grammar is based on the minimum necessary for understanding academic texts. The emphasis is largely on a general course content to cover common problems (such as reading strategies), rather than specific courses according to the student's subject specialism (e.g. "English for Engineers").'

a) Why do you think this approach has been adopted?
b) Do you think that the approach is a justifiable response to the needs of the students?
c) How do you think students and teachers will react to this approach?

3 ESP: approach not product

Beware that you do not lose the substance by grasping at the shadow.

(Aesop: 'The Fable of the Dog and the Shadow')

The survey above shows that in its relatively brief history there have been several major shifts in the development of ESP both in theory and practice. However, we have tried to show that, in spite of their differences, the successive stages have all concentrated on the linguistic aspect of ESP: they are all essentially language-centred approaches. In later chapters we shall look in greater detail at how this has shaped the way in which people see ESP. For now let us return to the question posed at the beginning of this section: 'What is ESP?' To answer this question fully, we need first of all to establish a context which will help us to see how ESP at the present time relates to the rest of ELT. What exactly is the status of the citizens of ESP and its satellite settlements in relation to the general world of ELT?

In the time-honoured manner of linguistics, we shall represent the relationship in the form of a tree (see figure 3).

The tree represents some of the common divisions that are made in ELT. The topmost branches of the tree show the level at which individual ESP courses occur. The branches just below this level indicate that these may conveniently be divided into two main types of ESP differentiated according to whether the learner requires English for academic study (EAP: English for Academic Purposes) or for work/ training (EOP/EVP/VESL: English for Occupational Purposes/English for Vocational Purposes/Vocational English as a Second Language). This is, of course, not a clear-cut distinction: people can work and study simultaneously; it is also likely that in many cases the language learnt for immediate use in a study environment will be used later when the student takes up, or returns to, a job.

At the next level down it is possible to distinguish ESP courses by the general nature of the learners' specialism. Three large categories are usually identified here: EST (English for Science and Technology), EBE (English for Business and Economics) and ESS (English for the Social Sciences). This last is not common, probably because it is not thought

16

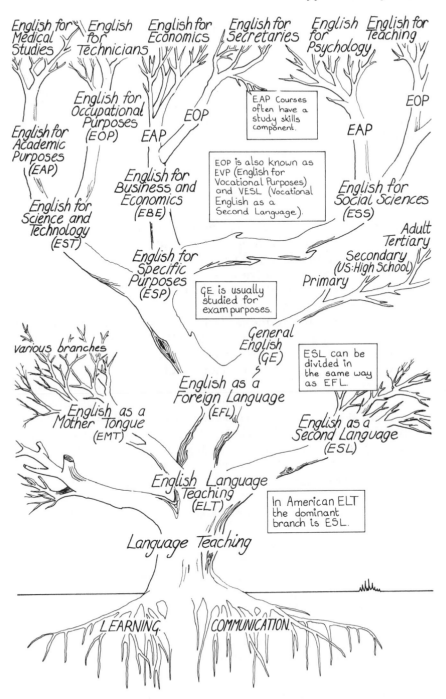

Figure 3: The tree of ELT

to differ significantly from more traditional humanities-based General English.

As we go down the tree, we can see that ESP is just one branch of EFL/ESL, which are themselves the main branches of English Language Teaching in general. ELT, in turn is one variety of the many possible kinds of language teaching.

But, of course, there is more to a tree than is visible above ground: a tree cannot survive without roots. The roots which nourish the tree of ELT are *communication* and *learning*.

The analogy of a tree can help us to get a bit closer to a definition of ESP not so much by showing what ESP is, but rather by showing what ESP isn't.

a) ESP is *not* a matter of teaching 'specialised varieties' of English. The fact that language is used for a specific purpose does *not* imply that it is a special form of the language, different in kind from other forms. Certainly, there are some features which can be identified as 'typical' of a particular context of use and which, therefore, the learner is more likely to meet in the target situation. But these differences should not be allowed to obscure the far larger area of common ground that underlies all English use, and indeed, all language use.

b) ESP is *not* just a matter of Science words and grammar for Scientists, Hotel words and grammar for Hotel staff and so on. When we look at a tree, we see the leaves and branches, but there is much more to the tree than just these – much of it hidden from view inside and beneath the tree. The leaves do not just hang in the air: they are supported by a complex underlying structure. In the same way there is much more to communication than just the surface features that we read and hear. We need to distinguish, as Chomsky did with regard to grammar, between *performance* and *competence*, that is between what people actually do with the language and the range of knowledge and abilities which enables them to do it (Hutchinson and Waters, 1981).

c) ESP is *not* different in kind from any other form of language teaching, in that it should be based in the first instance on principles of effective and efficient learning. Though the content of learning may vary there is no reason to suppose that the processes of learning should be any different for the ESP learner than for the General English learner. There is, in other words, no such thing as an ESP methodology, merely methodologies that have been applied in ESP classrooms, but could just as well have been used in the learning of any kind of English.

So what is ESP? Having stressed the commonality of language and learning, how does ESP differ from other forms of ELT? To answer this,

ESP must be seen as an *approach* not as a *product*. ESP is not a particular kind of language or methodology, nor does it consist of a particular type of teaching material. Understood properly, it is an approach to language learning, which is based on learner need. The foundation of all ESP is the simple question: Why does this learner need to learn a foreign language? From this question will flow a whole host of further questions, some of which will relate to the learners themselves, some to the nature of the language the learners will need to operate, some to the given learning context. But this whole analysis derives from an initial identified need on the part of the learner to learn a language. ESP, then, is an approach to language teaching in which all decisions as to content and method are based on the learner's reason for learning.

Conclusion

In this section we have identified the main factors in the origins of ESP and given a brief overview of its development. We have noted that the linguistic factor has tended to dominate this development with an emphasis on the analysis of the nature of specific varieties of language use. Probably this has been a necessary stage, but now there is a need for a wider view that focusses less on differences and more on what various specialisms have in common. As 'the tree of ELT' shows, what they have in common is that they are all primarily concerned with communication and learning. ESP should properly be seen not as any particular language product but as an approach to language teaching which is directed by specific and apparent reasons for learning.

Tasks

1 Our tree gives only a few examples of ESP courses. Complete the branches at the top, by adding other courses.

2 What differences would you expect to find between an EOP course and an EAP course for doctors? In what ways do you think occupational and academic needs differ?

3 All language teaching should be based on learner needs. Thus in theory there is no difference between ESP and General English teaching; in practice, however, there is a great deal of difference. How far would you agree with this statement? What differences, either in theory or in practice do you think there are?

Section 2   Course design

I keep six honest serving-men.
(They taught me all I knew.)
Their names are What and Why and When
And How and Where and Who.

(Rudyard Kipling)

We concluded the previous section by stating that ESP is an approach to language teaching which aims to meet the needs of particular learners. This means in practice that much of the work done by ESP teachers is concerned with designing appropriate courses for various groups of learners. Thus, whereas course design plays a relatively minor part in the life of the General English teacher – courses here usually being determined either by tradition, choice of textbook or ministerial decree – for the ESP teacher, course design is often a substantial and important part of the workload.

Designing a course is fundamentally a matter of asking questions in order to provide a reasoned basis for the subsequent processes of syllabus design, materials writing, classroom teaching and evaluation.

We need to ask a very wide range of questions: general and specific, theoretical and practical. Some of these questions will be answered (at least in part) by research; others will rely more on the intuition and experience of the teacher; yet others will call on theoretical models. We can use Kipling's 'honest serving men' to outline the basic questions. We need to know:

Why does the student need to learn?

Who is going to be involved in the process? This will need to cover not just the student, but all the people who may have some effect on the process: teachers, sponsors, inspectors etc.

Where is the learning to take place. What potential does the place provide? What limitations does it impose?

When is the learning to take place? How much time is available? How will it be distributed?

What does the student need to learn? What aspects of language will be needed and how will they be described? What level of proficiency must be achieved? What topic areas will need to be covered?

How will the learning be achieved? What learning theory will underlie the course? What kind of methodology will be employed?

In this section we shall investigate these basic questions more thoroughly, by considering them under three main headings: *Language descriptions, Theories of learning* and *Needs analysis*. We should emphasise, however, that, although for clarity we need to look at the three factors separately, it is their interdependence in the course design process which is of greatest importance. We might represent their relationship like this:

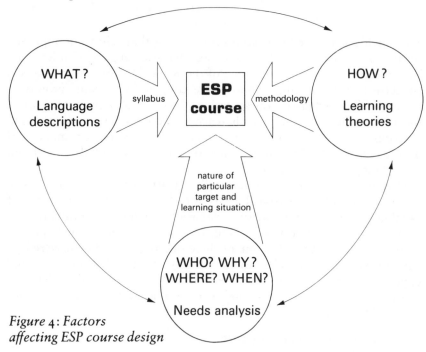

Figure 4: Factors affecting ESP course design

First a word about terminology: a lot of confusion is undoubtedly caused in discussions about ESP course design by the imprecise use of terms such as 'communicative', 'structural', 'functional' etc. Thus it is not uncommon to hear people talk of a 'functional approach' or a 'structural method', although no such things really exist; that much-abused term, 'communicative', is often used as if it were synonymous with 'functional', which it is not. To try and prevent such confusion, we shall adopt two strategies.

Firstly, wherever possible, we shall avoid the term 'communicative'.

This has become such an emotive word, that, rather like 'democracy' or 'freedom', it is claimed by everyone and is capable of innumerable interpretations, many of which are flatly contradictory. It has come, in effect, to mean simply a good, modern approach to language teaching, rather than indicating what that approach might consist of. Indeed, it is now almost an insult to infer that someone's materials or methods are uncommunicative. It is for this reason that we have taken in preference the term learning-centred, since it expresses more specifically what the principles of the approach are.

The second strategy we have adopted is to make a clear distinction between the two elements of *language description* and *learning theory*. The *language description* is the way in which the language system is broken down and described for the purposes of learning. Terms such as 'structural', 'functional', 'notional' properly belong to this area. They refer to ways of analysing and describing language. They say *nothing* about how the language items described can or should be taught. It is, therefore, inappropriate to use these terms in conjunction with 'approach' or 'method', since these latter terms indicate a way of, or attitude to, teaching. An approach or method derives not from a view of language, but from a view of learning. It is the *learning theory* which provides the theoretical basis for the methodology, by helping us to understand how people learn. It is also important to note that theories of learning are not necessarily confined to how people learn language, but can refer equally to the learning of any kind of knowledge, for example how to drive a car. In the area of learning theories the relevant terms we shall consider are 'behaviourist', 'cognitive', 'affective'.

Having clarified the terminology, we can proceed to a brief outline of this section. We stated in chapter 1 that ESP should be viewed in the broader context of ELT in general. Accordingly in chapters 4 and 5 we shall look at the main developments in *language descriptions* and *learning theory* in general terms and then consider how they have been, or can be, useful in ESP. In chapter 6 we shall consider *needs analysis*, arguing for a much broader concept of *needs* than is often defined. Finally in chapter 7 we shall describe various ways in which *language*, *learning* and *needs* have been dealt with in ESP course design.

Tasks

1 Our list of questions is very general. Take one of Kipling's 'honest serving-men' and make a detailed list of the questions you think it is important to ask as a preliminary to designing an ESP course.

2 What do you understand by the term 'communicative'? What features would, for example, characterise 'communicative' materials?

4 Language descriptions

> They have been at a great feast of language, and stolen the scraps.
>
> (Shakespeare: *Love's Labour's Lost*)

Any ESP course makes use of explicit or implicit ideas about the nature of language. These ideas are drawn from the various language descriptions that have been developed by succeeding schools of thought in Linguistics. We now have a number of ways of describing language available to us. It is, therefore, important to understand the main features of each of these descriptions in order to consider how they can be used most appropriately in ESP courses. Not all the developments in Linguistics have had pedagogic applications, of course. In this chapter we shall give a brief outline of the various ideas about language that have influenced ESP in some way. We can identify six main stages of development.

1 Classical or traditional grammar

Although language teaching has a long history stretching back to ancient times (see Howatt, 1984), the ways of describing language remained little changed until this century. Descriptions of English and other languages were based on the grammars of the classical languages, Greek and Latin. These descriptions were based on an analysis of the role played by each word in the sentence. Languages were described in this way because the classical languages were case-based languages where the grammatical function of each word in the sentence was made apparent by the use of appropriate inflections. Thus the form of a word would change according to whether it was a subject, object, indirect object and so on. The prestige of the old classical languages ensured the survival of this form of description even after English had lost most of its case markers and become a largely word-order based language.

Since ESP emerged after the classical form of description had been largely abandoned, its influence on ESP has never been strong. Nevertheless, it has continued to provide the teacher with a useful indirect source of guidance. Register analysis, for example, drew heavily upon its terminology in syllabus design (see p. 9). As Allen and Widdowson (1975) say:

'Teachers who wish to maintain a balanced view of linguistics should not overlook the fact that traditional grammar has many useful virtues. The traditional handbooks provided an array of terms and distinctions which most of us used in learning to talk about our own language, and which many people continue to find serviceable throughout their lives.'

It can also be argued that, although cases may no longer be apparent in modern English, the concepts they represent underlie any language (Fillmore, 1968). Thus a knowledge of the classical description can still deepen our knowledge of how languages operate.

2 Structural linguistics

The first real challenge to the classical description of languages came in the 1930s with the advent of structuralism, associated with linguists such as Bloomfield (1935). The structural or 'slot and filler' form of language description will be familiar to most language teachers as a result of the enormous influence it has had on language teaching since the Second World War.

In a structural description the grammar of the language is described in terms of syntagmatic structures which carry the fundamental propositions (statement, interrogative, negative, imperative etc.) and notions (time, number, gender etc.). By varying the words within these structural frameworks, sentences with different meanings can be generated. This method of linguistic analysis led in English language teaching to the development of the substitution table as a typical means of explaining grammatical patterns. These are still widely used today as this example from the Nucleus series shows:

5. Write nine sentences from this table. Remember that there are many different possibilities, not just nine correct sentences.

Diabetes mellitus			unconsciousness.
Inadequate heat loss		cause	shock.
Some foods			bad teeth.
A dog bite			death.
An electric shock	can	result in	heat stroke.
Insufficient calcium	may		blisters.
Severe shock			allergies.
Burns		lead to	asphyxia.
A haemorrhage			rabies.

(from *Nucleus: Nursing Science* by R. Kerr and J. Smith, Longman, 1978)

Figure 5: A substitution table in ESP

In fact, the development of structural descriptions of languages had little to do with English in its early stages, but came from the need to describe the Indian languages of North America before the last native speakers died. It soon became apparent, however, that for a word-order language such as English the slot and filler description would also be particularly appropriate.

Apart from the substitution table, the most enduring application of structural linguistics was the structural syllabus, which has proved to be a very powerful means of selecting and sequencing language items. In such a syllabus, items are graded so that simpler and more immediately useable structures precede the more complex ones. An example of an ESP syllabus based on structural precepts is that used by Ewer and Latorre (1969) (minor details omitted):

1 Simple Present Active
2 Simple Present Passive
3 Simple Present Active and Passive
4 -ing forms
5 Present Perfect; Present Continuous
6 Infinitives
7 Anomalous Finites
8 Past Perfect; Conditionals

At its best the structural syllabus provides the learner with a systematic description of the generative core of the language – the finite range of structures that make it possible to generate an infinite number of novel utterances. For this reason the structural syllabus continues to be widely used in spite of criticism from advocates of functional, notional or use-based descriptions of English (see e.g. Wilkins, 1976 and Widdowson, 1979). Its strength is also its greatest weakness. The very simplicity of the structural language description entails that there are large areas of language use that it cannot explain. In particular it may fail to provide the learner with an understanding of the communicative use of the structures (Allen and Widdowson, 1974). Later developments in language teaching and linguistics have attempted to remedy this weakness.

3 Transformational Generative (TG) grammar

The structural view of language as a collection of syntagmatic patterns held sway until the publication in 1957 of *Syntactic Structures* by Noam Chomsky. Chomsky argued that the structural description was too superficial, because it only described the surface structure of the language, and thus could not explain relationships of meaning which were quite clearly there, but which were not realised in the surface structure. Thus these two sentences:

John is easy to please.
John is eager to please.

would, according to a structural description, indicate the same relationship between the words in the sentences. But obviously the relationship is not the same: in the first sentence John is the receiver of pleasing, while in the second he is doing the pleasing. Similarly the identity of meaning between an active and passive sentence would not be shown, e.g.

The City Bank has taken over Acme Holdings.
Acme Holdings has been taken over by the City Bank.

Here the relationships of meaning within the two sentences are identical, but in a structural description this cannot be shown. Structurally they are different and there is no way of indicating the identity of meaning.

Chomsky concluded that these problems arose because language was being analysed and described in isolation from the human mind which produces it. He maintained that, if we want to understand how language works, it cannot be viewed as a phenomenon in itself. It must be viewed as a reflection of human thought patterns. He proposed that there must be two levels of meaning: a deep level, which is concerned with the organisation of thoughts and a surface level, where these thoughts are expressed through the syntax of the language. The grammar of a language is, therefore, not the surface structures themselves, but the rules that enable the language user to generate the surface structures from the deep level of meaning.

Chomsky's work had an enormous and direct influence on the world of Linguistics. His effect on language teaching has been more indirect, but no less important. Firstly he re-established the idea that language is rule-governed. (We shall consider this aspect in more detail under learning theories in chapter 5.) Secondly, he widened the view of language to incorporate the relationship between meaning and form. This second aspect had a considerable influence on language teaching through the next school of thought that we shall describe. But for ESP the most important lesson to be drawn from Chomsky's work was the distinction he made between *performance* (i.e. the surface structures) and *competence* (i.e. the deep level rules). Chomsky's own definition of performance and competence was narrowly based, being concerned only with syntax. In ESP we need to take a much broader view, but the basic distinction itself is still valid. Put simply, describing what people *do* with the language (performance) is important, but of equal, if not greater importance is discovering the competence that *enables them to do* it (Hutchinson and Waters, 1981).

A simple way of seeing the distinction between performance and competence is in our capacity to understand the meanings of words we have never met before. For example, the expression 'multangular tower' occurs in a widely used English test. It is a word most people will never have seen. But, if you know the prefix 'multi' (whether in your own language or English), the word 'angle' and the basic word formation rules of English, it is an easy matter to work out that a 'multangular tower' is a many-sided tower, that is, not a round or a square one (see also p. 140). This process of interpretation would not be possible unless there were an underlying competence which can operate separately from the performance features of the language.

In the early stages of its development, ESP put most emphasis on describing the performance needed for communication in the target situation and paid little attention to the competence underlying it. Indeed, accustomed as we are to seeing language and language learning in terms of performance, it can be difficult to grasp the importance of the competence/performance distinction. But it is one of crucial importance for ESP and we shall return to it in the ensuing chapters. As we have argued elsewhere:

'We need to make a distinction between the performance repertoire of the target situation and the competence required to cope with it. The competence, providing, as it does, the generative basis for further learning... is the proper concern of ESP.' (*ibid.*)

In the developments we have described so far we have considered language solely from the point of view of *form*. But language does not exist for its own sake. It exists because people do things with it: they give information; they promise; they threaten; they make excuses; they seek information; they classify; they identify; they report. Language, in other words, can also be looked at from the point of view of *function*, that is, what people do with it. This is not a new idea. The British sociolinguist, J. R. Firth, investigated language in this way in the 1930s. But it only became an important movement in Linguistics with the development of the concept of 'communicative competence'. Sociolinguists, such as Dell Hymes, proposed that competence consists not just of a set of rules for formulating grammatically correct sentences, but also a knowledge of 'when to speak, when not...what to talk about with whom, when, where, in what manner.' (Hymes, 1972) The study of language in use, therefore, should look not just at syntax, but also at the other ingredients of communication, such as: non-verbal communication (gesture, posture, eye contact etc.), the medium and channel of communication, role relationships between the participants, the topic and purpose of communication.

The concept of communicative competence has had far-reaching consequences for ESP. It led to the next three stages of development which we shall consider: language variation and register analysis; language as function; discourse analysis.

4 Language variation and register analysis

Consider these two texts. They are both describing the same job: drilling a hole in a metal workpiece on a lathe. Text A is a transcript from a video-taped demonstration in using the lathe. Text B is a set of instructions taken from a workshop manual.

TEXT A

Now I have to change to the final size drill I require, which is three-quarters of an inch diameter, and this is called a morse-taper sleeve.

A slower speed for a larger drill.

Nice even feed should give a reasonable finish to the hole.

Applying coolant periodically. This is mainly for lubrication rather than cooling.

Almost to depth now.
Right. Withdrawing the drill.

That's fine.

TEXT B

1 Select required drill.
2 Mount drill in tailstock. Use taper sleeves as necessary.
3 Set speed and start machine spindle.
4 Position tailstock to workpiece.
5 Apply firm even pressure to tailstock handwheel to feed drill into workpiece.
6 Apply coolant frequently.
7 Drill hole to depth.
8 Withdraw drill.
9 Stop machine.

(Hutchinson and Waters, 1981)

The illocutionary force of these two texts is the same, that is to say they are both conveying the same message and they both have the same purpose, namely to give instructions in carrying out the particular job. But the language of text A differs from that of text B in a number of significant ways:

a) In A the speaker is not giving a direct set of instructions. He is actually commenting on what he is doing, but this functions as a set of instructions.

b) The language is more anecdotal and sporadic. This is because there is a visual element to the discourse. The main thrust of the communication is carried by what he is doing with the machine (Hutchinson, 1978).

c) In text A there is an interpersonal dimension. The language is, therefore, less formal and contains some comments and expressions of feeling, for example, 'That's fine.'

d) The grammar of text B is consistent (e.g. the articles are always omitted; the verb form is always the imperative). In text A there is less consistency, because it is a free-flowing piece of spoken discourse.

There are other differences too, but our purpose is not to give a detailed analysis. The important point is that, if we view language as part of a communicative whole, it is clear that language use shows considerable variety. The whole communicative act is made up of a number of contextually dependent factors. Varying one or more of these factors will have 'knock-on' effects on the other factors. Thus the presence of the machine in text A affects what needs to be said in order to convey the message. This sentence, 'and this is called a morse-taper sleeve' is only possible, because the audience can see both the object referred to and the speaker's actions which indicate that it is being referred to. Language, then, varies according to the context of use and it is this fact that enables us to distinguish, for example, formal from informal, written from spoken, self-sufficient language from context-dependent.

The concept of language variation gave rise to the type of ESP which was based on register analysis (see above p. 9). If language varies according to context, it was argued, then it should be possible to identify the kind of language associated with a specific context, such as an area of knowledge (legal English; social English; medical English; business English; scientific English etc.), or an area of use (technical manuals, academic texts, business meetings, advertisements, doctor-patient communication etc.). Much ESP research was focussed as a result on determining the formal characteristics of various registers in order to establish a basis for the selection of syllabus items. The work of Ewer and Latorre (1969) and Swales (1971) on the language of science was particularly significant here. However, register analysis has, as we have already noted, ultimately proved to be an insubstantial basis for the selection of syllabus items. As Coffey (1984) says about EST:

'Research and experiment continue, but in general the results have not been encouraging... In short, register cannot be used as a main basis for selection, because there is no significant way in which the language of science differs from any other kind of language.'

The key phrase here is 'no significant way'. There are clearly language forms that tend to be used more frequently in one context than in another. The classic example of this is the use of the passive in Scientific English. But even this may have been overemphasised. Tarone *et al.* (1981) found in their analysis of two Astrophysics journal papers that the active accounted for over 80% of the verbs used. But the important point is that even if particular registers favour certain forms, they are not distinctive forms. They are simply drawn from the common stock of the grammar of the language. Though attractive at first sight, the assumption that language variation implies the existence of identifiable varieties of language related to specific contexts of use has, in effect, proved to be unfounded.

5 Functional/Notional grammar

The second major offshoot of work into language as communication which has influenced ESP has been the functional/notional concept of language description. The terms 'functional' and 'notional' are easily and frequently confused. There is, however, a difference. Functions are concerned with social behaviour and represent the intention of the speaker or writer, for example, advising, warning, threatening, describing etc. They can be approximately equated with the communicative acts that are carried out through language. Notions, on the other hand, reflect the way in which the human mind thinks. They are the categories into which the mind and thereby language divides reality, for example, time, frequency, duration, gender, number, location, quantity, quality etc. (see e.g. Johnson and Morrow, 1981, pp. 1–11).

The functional view of language began to have an influence on language teaching in the 1970s, largely as a result of the Council of Europe's efforts to establish some kind of equivalence in the syllabuses for learning various languages. Equivalence was difficult to establish on formal grounds, since the formal structures of languages show considerable variation. The student of German, for example, is likely to have to spend a large amount of time in learning the gender/case endings of articles, nouns and adjectives. The learner of English on the other hand will not have this problem, but may need to spend more time on, for example, the spelling, the simple/continuous tense distinction or the countable/uncountable distinction. These variations in the formal features of languages obviously make it difficult to divide up the learning tasks into units of equivalent value across the various languages on the basis of formal grammar. On notional or functional grounds, however, some approximate equivalence can be achieved, since notions and functions represent the categories of human thinking and social behaviour, which do not (as far as we know) vary across languages. Thus in the 1970s there was a move from language syllabuses organised on structural grounds to ones based on functional or notional criteria. The most influential of such syllabuses were the Threshold Level (Van Ek, 1975) and Waystage (Van Ek and Alexander, 1977) syllabuses produced by the Council of Europe.

The move towards functionally based syllabuses has been particularly strong in the development of ESP, largely on the pragmatic grounds that the majority of ESP students have already done a structurally organised syllabus, probably at school. Their needs, therefore, are not to learn the basic grammar, but rather to learn how to use the knowledge they already have.

The attraction of the functional syllabus is that it appears to be based on language in use, in contrast to the structural syllabus, which shows only form. For example, compare this syllabus with the Ewer and Latorre syllabus above (p. 26):

Asking about travel
Making travel arrangements
Ordering a meal
Asking the way
Hiring a car

(from *English for Travel* by John Eastwood, OUP, 1980)

(See pp. 85–8 for various types of syllabus.)

The functional syllabus, however, has its own drawbacks. It suffers in particular from a lack of any kind of systematic conceptual framework, and as such does not help the learners to organise their knowledge of the language.

The main problem with the functional syllabus, however, is not the syllabus itself, but the fact that it is too often seen as a replacement for the older structural syllabus. A more constructive approach to describing language in structural or functional terms is to see the two as complementary, with each supporting and enriching the other. The relationship between the two can be best expressed in the form of this simple equation:

structure + context = function

Brumfit (1981) proposes a similar approach with his 'snakes and ladders' syllabus. A core ladder of structures is intertwined with a spiralling snake of related functions. An example of this kind of syllabus can be seen in more recent ESP materials (see figure 6).

Contents

Unit One	A visitor to BOS	**Page 1**
Business content:	Organisation chart	
Structures:	The verb *to be* Possessive pronouns Genitive ('s) Question words: *What? Where? Who?*	
Functions:	Introductions; greetings; giving personal information; registering at a hotel	
Lexis:	Jobs, countries, nationalities, titles	
Unit Two	A newcomer	**Page 9**
Business content:	Telephone conversations; business letter format	
Structures:	Demonstrative pronouns: *this/that/these/those* *There is/there are* Prepositions: *on, in, above, below, under, between, next to, to the left/right of, on the right/left* Question words: *How many?*	
Function:	Describing location	
Lexis:	Office furniture and equipment, stationery, cardinal numbers, business letter teminology	
Unit Three	The BOS building	**Page 18**
Business content:	A memorandum; telephone conversations; company names	
Structures:	Present progressive tense Imperatives Prepositions (*continued*) Question word: *Which?*	
Functions:	Discussing activities; giving directions; giving commands	
Lexis:	Ordinal numbers, parts of a building, some office activities	

(from *We Mean Business* by Susan Norman, Longman, 1982)

Figure 6: A structural/functional syllabus

6 Discourse (Rhetorical) analysis

This next development has also had a profound effect on ESP. Till this point language had been viewed in terms of the sentence. Now the emphasis moved to looking at how meaning is generated *between* sentences. This was a logical development of the functional/notional view of language which had shown that there is more to meaning than just the words in the sentence. The context of the sentence is also important in creating the meaning.

If we take this simple sentence: 'It is raining' and we put it into three different dialogues, we can see how the meaning changes.

Can I go out to play?
It's raining.

Have you cut the grass yet?
It's raining.

I think I'll go out for a walk.
It's raining.

In each case the propositional meaning (statement) of the sentence is the same. The notions in it are also the same (present time, neuter). But the sentence is fulfilling three different communicative purposes.

In the first dialogue a parent could be talking to a child. The child is asking permission to go out. The parent's reply of 'It is raining' acts as a refusal of the request. The second dialogue might be a husband/wife dialogue. 'It is raining' now functions as a reason or an excuse. In the third dialogue it takes on yet another function, and this time is probably acting as advice or a mild warning and might take place between friends.

The meaning of this same sentence changes with the different contexts. This change is brought about by two factors. The first factor, as we have seen, is the sociolinguistic context: who is speaking to whom and why. The meaning changes according to the relationship between the participants in the dialogue and according to their reason for speaking. But there is another factor which influences the meaning – the relative positions of the utterances within the discourse. An utterance acquires meaning by virtue of what utterances it precedes or follows. We might call this the discoursal meaning.

For example, if we take the third dialogue above and turn the two utterances round, we get:

It's raining.
I think I'll go out for a walk.

By doing so, we have first of all removed the idea of advice or warning. We have also completely changed the logical meaning of the dialogue. In the first example the underlying meaning is that rain provides a reason *against* going for a walk, whereas in the reversed example rain is a reason *in favour of* going out for a walk. Thus the relative positions of the utterances within the discourse affect the meaning of the discourse.

As we noted in chapter 2, discourse analysis has been closely associated with ESP, particularly through the influence of Henry Widdowson and the Washington School of American linguists. We can identify two key ways in which the results of studies into the nature of discourse have been used in ESP teaching materials:

a) Learners are made aware of the stages in certain set-piece transactions associated with particular specialist fields. One of the most influential projects of this kind has been the analysis of doctor-patient communication by Candlin, Bruton and Leather (1976). A similar approach can be seen in the following example (see figure 7).

b) The second use of discourse analysis in ESP has been through materials which aim to explain how meaning is created by the relative

2 The form of a consultation

Objective: To examine the sequence of a consultation.

The form of a consultation

The conversation between Mr Watson and Mr Finbury, like most consultations in a bank, was of the following form.

1 *Establishing contact.* The manager or assistant manager first establishes contact with his customer, greeting him and putting him at his ease. This is done politely, but with neither effusiveness or familiarity.

2 *Finding out what the person wants.* It's necessary to find out what the client wants.

3 *Giving information.* Information is given concisely, vividly and clearly. Moreover, it is adapted to the listener's viewpoint.

4 *Arguing the point.* The client is persuaded to do something.

5 *Taking down details in writing.* Very often it will be necessary to fill in a form or take notes.

6 *Conclusion and thanks.* The manager reaffirms his readiness to help.

Look at the text of the dialogue on pp. 4-6, and mark where each section begins and ends.

(from *English for International Banking* by Ferguson and O'Reilly, Evans, 1979)

Figure 7: Discourse analysis in ESP

positions of the sentences in a written text. This has become the central feature of a large number of ESP textbooks aimed at developing a knowledge of how sentences are combined in texts in order to produce a particular meaning (Allen and Widdowson, 1974). This approach has led, in particular, to the text-diagramming type of exercise found in many ESP materials. The ultimate aim of such an approach is to make the learners into more efficient readers, by making them aware of the underlying structure of a text and the way in which language has been organised to create this structure. The following extract from *Reading and Thinking in English: Exploring Functions* is an example of the text-diagramming type of exercise.

Unit 6   GENERALIZING AND EXEMPLIFYING

b   uses of natural materials
c   uses of man-made materials
d   the advantages of natural materials.

The two dominant factors which determine the use of a material are its cost and its physical and chemical properties.[11]   The specificaions of the designers have to be matched against what is known about a material's strength, how easily it conducts electricity, how quickly it corrodes, etc.[12]   But the material chosen for a given application is the one which most cheaply meets the specifications of the designers.[13]   Even when special materials have to be developed to meet a particular specification, the costs of production have to be carefully controlled.

[11] What does the use of a material depend on?

[12] The material's strength, etc. are examples of . . . . . .

[13] Which material is chosen?

meet = satisfy

material which meets the specifications:
a   £50
b   £20
c   £15 ← choice

9   Complete the following table to summarize the paragraph.

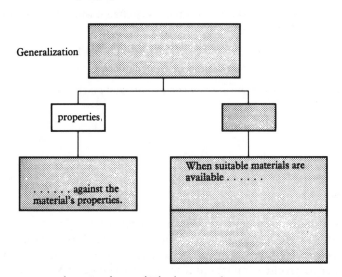

(from *Reading and Thinking: Exploring Functions*, OUP, 1979)

Figure 8: Text-diagramming

Even before *Reading and Thinking* was published, the approach had come under attack on the grounds that it misrepresents the real nature of discourse. It has been suggested (see, in particular, Coulthard (1977) pp. 147–53) that the approach does for discourse what structural linguistics did for sentence grammar, in other words, it establishes patterns, but does not account for how these patterns create meaning. It has produced, in effect, a sort of discourse structuralism. It can also be argued that it falls into the very same trap that Allen and Widdowson (1974) claimed to be trying to remedy. If getting learners to learn structural sentence patterns does not enable the learner to use those patterns in communication, is it any more likely that making learners aware of the patterns in discourse will enable them to use those discourse patterns in communication? Are not descriptions of language *use* being taken for descriptions of language *learning*? We shall return to this theme in the following chapters, when we consider the fields of learning and needs.

Conclusion

We have looked in this chapter at the ways in which language can be, and has been, described. There are three lessons to be learnt from this survey and they must be borne in mind when we draw conclusions regarding their relevance to ESP course design:

a) There is no single source from which a language course can, or should, derive its linguistic input. The various developments which we have described are not separate entities. Each stage has reacted to, and drawn inspiration from, those preceding it. A functional description does not imply that a structural description is wrong, simply that it is not sufficient as an explanation of what language is like. The ESP teacher needs to recognise that the various approaches are different ways of looking at the *same* thing. All communication has a structural level, a functional level and a discoursal level. They are not mutually exclusive, but complementary, and each may have its place in the ESP course.

b) Describing a language for the purposes of linguistic analysis does not necessarily carry any implications for language learning. The purposes of the linguist and of the language teacher are not the same. Stern (1983) sounds a note of caution, which ESP practitioners would do well to heed:

'Whether techniques of linguistic analysis – however well they may lend themselves to linguistic research – are equally applicable to language teaching is of course open to question.'

c) Describing a language is not the same as describing what enables someone to use or learn a language. We must make a distinction between what a person does (*performance*) and what enables them to do it (*competence*). Similarly we must not confuse how people *use* a language with how people *learn* it.

The importance of these points can only be fully appreciated when we consider the psychological processes that lie behind language use and language learning. In the next chapter we shall consider this dimension by describing developments in learning theories and their implications for ESP.

Tasks

1 Do you think that classical and structural descriptions still have a value in ESP? Why?

2 What do you think is the importance of the concept of communicative competence in ESP?

3 Continue the analysis of texts A and B on p. 29. What further differences can you see? Account for the differences.

4 Look at the dialogues on pp. 33–4. What knowledge enables us to interpret them? How are we able to imagine a context for them?

5 Look at the extract from *Reading and Thinking* (p. 36).
a) What are the exercises trying to teach?
b) What sort of learners do you think would benefit from this material?

6 In what ways do the interests of linguistic research and language teaching differ?

5 Theories of learning

Give a man a fish and you feed him for a day.
Teach a man how to fish and you feed him for a lifetime.

(Chinese proverb)

The starting point for all language teaching should be an understanding of how people learn. But it is too often the case that 'learning' factors are the last to be considered. ESP has been particularly guilty in this regard. As we saw in the previous chapter, the overwhelming weight of emphasis in ESP research and materials has been on language analysis. Learning factors, if considered at all, are incorporated only after the language base has been analysed and systematised (see Munby, 1978 p. 217). We have, in effect, been more concerned with arriving than with the journey.

Yet, language can only be properly understood as a reflection of human thought processes. Language learning is conditioned by the way in which the mind observes, organises and stores information. In other words, the key to successful language learning and teaching lies not in the analysis of the nature of language but in understanding the structure and processes of the mind. Unfortunately, we still know too little about how people learn. Nevertheless, if we wish to improve the techniques, methods and content of language teaching, we must try and base what we do in the classroom on sound principles of learning.

Developments in learning theory have followed a similar pattern to those in language descriptions, and each has had some effect on the other. But, if we are to see the importance of each for language teaching, it is best to consider the theories relating to language and learning separately. As with language descriptions, we shall describe the main developments in theories of how learners learn and relate each to the needs of the ESP learner and teacher.

Until the twentieth century there was no coherent theory of learning available to the language teacher. Certainly there were empirical observations, such as Comenius' studies made in the sixteenth century and the precepts of the Direct Method at the end of the nineteenth century (see e.g. Stern, 1983). But no coherent theory of learning emerged until psychology had been established as a respectable subject of

39

scientific enquiry in the early twentieth century. We can identify five main stages of development since then, which are of relevance to the modern language teacher (see Littlewood, 1984, for an excellent survey of theories of learning).

1 Behaviourism: learning as habit formation

The first coherent theory of learning was the behaviourist theory based mainly on the work of Pavlov in the Soviet Union and of Skinner in the United States. This simple but powerful theory said that learning is a mechanical process of habit formation and proceeds by means of the frequent reinforcement of a stimulus-response sequence.

The simplicity and directness of this theory had an enormous impact on learning psychology and on language teaching. It provided the theoretical underpinning of the widely used Audiolingual Method of the 1950s and 1960s. This method, which will be familiar to many language teachers, laid down a set of guiding methodological principles, based firstly on the behaviourist stimulus-response concept and secondly on an assumption that second language learning should reflect and imitate the perceived processes of mother tongue learning. Some of these precepts were:

Never translate.
New language should always be dealt with in the sequence: hear, speak, read, write.
Frequent repetition is essential to effective learning.
All errors must be immediately corrected.

The basic exercise technique of a behaviourist methodology is pattern practice, particularly in the form of language laboratory drills. Such drills are still widely used in ESP, as we can see in these two examples from textbooks for scientific English and business English:

drill 2

The liquid was heated. When the temperature reached 100°C, the heating was stopped.
The liquid was heated until the temperature reached 100°C.

The material was stretched. When it was 50 cm long, the stretching was stopped.
The material was stretched until it was 50 cm long.

(from *Basic English for Science* by Peter Donovan, OUP, 1978)

D2 Drill

Who's Dr Walker?
She's a consultant, isn't she?

Who does Manuel Silva work for?
He works for the NDA, doesn't he?

1. consultant
2. the NDA
3. EAU
4. power stations
5. German
6. silicon
7. guaranteed market
8. one watt

(from *Bid for Power* by A. Fitzpatrick and C. St J. Yates, BBC, 1983)

Figure 9: ESP language drills

Modern ESP books have also looked for more interesting ways of handling pattern practice and a number of useful variations on the basic idea have been developed. In particular, authors have tried to provide a meaningful context for the drills, as this example from an American ESP course shows:

EXERCISE 2 · DIFFERENT WAYS TO GIVE YOUR QUALIFICATIONS

A. There are several different ways to give your qualifications.

Read the examples. Then practice what an applicant might say for each job.

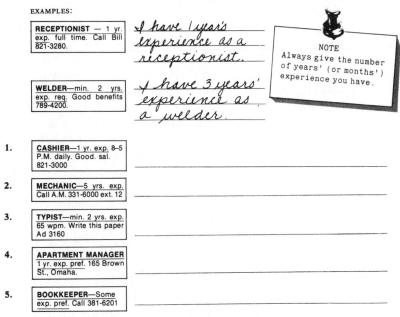

(from *It's Up to You* by J. Dresner, K. Beck, C. Morgano and L. Custer, Longman Inc., 1980)

Figure 10: A language drill: variation on a theme

Pattern practice exercises still have a useful role to play in language teaching (see chapter 10), but only as one part of the whole learning process. Under the Audiolingual Method they constituted almost the entire methodology. Subsequent developments have, as we shall see, shown that learning is much more complex than just imitative habit formation. But this does not necessarily mean that there is *no* place for pattern practice in a modern methodology (see e.g. Stevick, 1982). The mistake is to see it as the only kind of activity required.

2 Mentalism: thinking as rule-governed activity

There was considerable empirical evidence among language teachers that the Audiolingual Method and its behaviourist principles did not deliver the results promised. For apparently perverse reasons, language learners would not conform to the behaviourist stereotype: they insisted on translating things, asked for rules of grammar, found repeating things to a tape recorder boring, and somehow failed to learn something no matter how often they repeated it (see Allwright, 1984a). Such evidence from the classrooms, however, did little to diminish the influence of the theory – a sad example of human mistrust of intuition and experience in favour of theory!

The first successful assault on the behaviourist theory came from Chomsky (1964). He tackled behaviourism on the question of how the mind was able to transfer what was learnt in one stimulus-response sequence to other novel situations. There was a vague concept of 'generalisation' in behaviourist theory, but this was always skated over and never properly explained. Chomsky dismissed the generalisation idea as unworkable, because it simply could not explain how from a finite range of experience, the human mind was able to cope with an infinite range of possible situations. His conclusion was that thinking must be rule-governed: a finite, and fairly small, set of rules enables the mind to deal with the potentially infinite range of experiences it may encounter.

Having established thinking as rule-governed behaviour, it is one short step to the conclusion that learning consists not of forming habits but of acquiring rules – a process in which individual experiences are used by the mind to formulate a hypothesis. This hypothesis is then tested and modified by subsequent experience. The mind, in other words, does not just respond to a stimulus, it uses the individual stimuli in order to find the underlying pattern or system. It can then use this knowledge of the system in a novel situation to predict what is likely to happen, what is an appropriate response or whatever.

The mentalist view of the mind as a rule-seeker led naturally to the next important stage – the cognitive theory of learning.

3 Cognitive code: learners as thinking beings

Whereas the behaviourist theory of learning portrayed the learner as a passive receiver of information, the cognitive view takes the learner to be an active processor of information (see e.g. Ausubel *et al.*, 1978). Learning and using a rule require learners to think, that is, to apply their mental powers in order to distil a workable generative rule from the mass of data presented, and then to analyse the situations where the application of the rule would be useful or appropriate. Learning, then, is a process in which the learner actively tries to make sense of data, and learning can be said to have taken place when the learner has managed to impose some sort of meaningful interpretation or pattern on the data. This may sound complex, but in simple terms what it means is that we learn by thinking about and trying to make sense of what we see, feel and hear.

The basic teaching technique associated with a cognitive theory of language learning is the problem-solving task. In ESP such exercises have often been modelled on activities associated with the learners' subject specialism. The following from the Nucleus series is a representative example:

9. Now read this passage:

The factors affecting the rate of heat transfer through the skin also determine the rate of diffusion of gases through the walls of the cells, tissues and organs of plants and animals. For example, oxygen and carbon dioxide are absorbed through the walls of various organs. The greater the surface area of these organs in relation to their volume, the more of the surface will be exposed to the gas, and hence the faster the rate of diffusion.

The following examples illustrate the effects of the surface area/volume ratio on heat transfer and diffusion. Explain them by answering the questions:

a) Cold-blooded animals depend on the warmth of the sun to make their muscles work. The wings of butterflies and the tails of reptiles serve to absorb warmth. Why is this?

b) The smallest humming-bird weighs less than 2 grams. Why are humming-birds only found in hot countries?

⟫→

43

c) In hot weather, hippopotamuses and water buffaloes spend a lot of time in the water. Why do they have to do this?

d) Why do animals sleep curled up in cold weather but stretched out in warm weather?

e) Why are aquatic warm-blooded animals in northern and southern seas very large? (whales, seals, dolphins)

f) Why do babies suffer more from the cold than adults?
g) Why are leaves broad and flat?
h) Why are human lungs shaped like this?

i) Why don't micro-organisms need special organs for the absorption of oxygen?

(from *Nucleus*: *Biology*, D. Adamson and M. Bates, Longman, 1976)

Figure 11: *Problem-solving activities*

More recently, the cognitive view of learning has had a significant impact on ESP through the development of courses to teach reading strategies. A number of ESP projects (see above p. 13) have concentrated on making students aware of their reading strategies so that they can consciously apply them to understanding texts in a foreign language (see e.g. Alderson, 1980 and Scott, 1981). The following examples were produced for the University of Malaya ESP Project:

Activity A (35 minutes)	Do you need a dictionary? (1)
Specific Aim	To give students practice in deciding whether or not to use a dictionary in the context of reading a text for particular purposes.

1 The format for this activity has been chosen for the following reasons:

(a) to make reading purposeful;
(b) to highlight the issue of relevance;

(c)   to allow for individual variations in language proficiency
different words are unknown to different students;
students vary in their ability to use contextual clues, etc.

2   The student should therefore emerge from this lesson with a
knowledge not of what words he needs to look up but of what issues
he needs to bear in mind in deciding whether or not he should look
up a word in a dictionary:

(a)   Is the meaning of the unknown word *relevant* to my needs?

(b)   If it is *relevant,* is it *necessary,* ie can I get the same information
from other words in the text?

(c)   Is a *generic* meaning enough or do I need the *precise* meaning of
the word, ie how much guessing can I get away with?

(d)   How can I arrive at the meaning of the word without having to
look it up in a dictionary?

Make sure you keep all these points in mind as you handle the lesson.

The Major Processes of an Economic System

Four major processes cover the activities of people in any economic system:
the primary raw material industries, manufacturing, distribution, and the
service industries. First there is the process that provides the raw materials
needed in a modern economy: the minerals and fuels; the grains and other
vegetable and animal food products; wool, cotton, flax, and other fibres;
lumber; stone, sand and clay; leather, hides, and skin and like commodities.
This is the work of enterprises engaged in agriculture, mining, lumbering,
hunting, and fishing — often called the extractive, or primary industries.

Yes No

| | | (a)   Is a fibre a kind of raw material?

| | | (b)   Is silk a kind of fibre?

| | | (c)   Is lumber another name for fibre?

| | | (d)   Is lumbering an extractive industry?

| | | (e)   Is cutting down trees an extractive industry?

Activity D
●●

Choose the appropriate reference

Here is a bibliography on polymerization.

Decide which of the publications in the list are likely to give you (a) a brief
introduction to the subject; (b) an account of current developments in the
field; (c) an historical perspective on the subject; (d) the opinions of several
writers on the subject. Note down your answers.

1   Billmeyer, F. W. *Textbook of Polymer Science.* New York: John Willey
and Sons, 1962.

2   *The Condensed Chemical Dictionary.*

3 *Encyclopaedia Britannica.*

4 *International Encyclopaedia of Science.*

5 Lappert. M. F., and Leigh. G. J., ed., *Developments in Inorganic Polymer Chemistry.* New York: American Elsevier Publishing Co., 1962.

6 Mandelkern, Leo. *An Introduction to Macromolecules.* New York: Springer-Verlag, 1972.

7 Mark, H. F. *"The Nature of Polymeric Materials."* Scientific American, September 1967, p. 149.

8 Morton, Maurice. *"Polymers Ten Years Later."* Chemistry, October 1974, pp. 11–14.

9 Slabaugh, H. W., and Parsons, T. D. *General Chemistry.* New York: Wiley and Sons Inc., 1971.

10 Stille, J. K. *Introduction to Polymer Chemistry.* New York: John Wiley and Sons, 1962.

11 Wasserman, Leonard G. *Chemistry: Basic Concepts and Contemporary Applications.* Belmont, California: Wadsworth Publishing Company Inc., 1974.

(from *ELT Documents* 107: *The University of Malaya English for Special Purposes project (UMESPP*, British Council, 1980).

Figure 12: Reading strategies tasks

The cognitive code view of learning seems to answer many of the theoretical and practical problems raised by behaviourism. It treats the learners as thinking beings and puts them firmly at the centre of the learning process, by stressing that learning will only take place when the matter to be learnt is meaningful to the learners. But in itself a cognitive view is not sufficient. To complete the picture we need an affective view too.

4 The affective factor: learners as emotional beings

People think, but they also have feelings. It is one of the paradoxes of human nature that, although we are all aware of our feelings and their effects on our actions, we invariably seek answers to our problems in rational terms. It is as if we believed that human beings always act in a logical and sensible manner. This attitude affects the way we see learners – more like machines to be programmed ('I've taught them the past tense. They must know it.') than people with likes and dislikes, fears, weaknesses and prejudices. But learners are people. Even ESP learners are people. They may be learning *about* machines and systems, but they still learn *as* human beings. Learning, particularly the learning of a language, is an emotional experience, and the feelings that the learning process evokes will have a crucial bearing on the success or failure of the learning (see e.g. Stevick, 1976).

The importance of the emotional factor is easily seen if we consider the relationship between the cognitive and affective aspects of the learner. The cognitive theory tells us that learners will learn when they actively think about what they are learning. But this cognitive factor presupposes the affective factor of motivation. Before learners can actively think about something, they must *want* to think about it. The emotional reaction to the learning experience is the essential foundation for the initiation of the cognitive process. *How* the learning is perceived by the learner will affect *what* learning, if any, will take place.

We can represent the cognitive/affective interplay in the form of a learning cycle. This can either be a negative or a positive cycle. A good and appropriate course will engender the kind of positive learning cycle represented here:

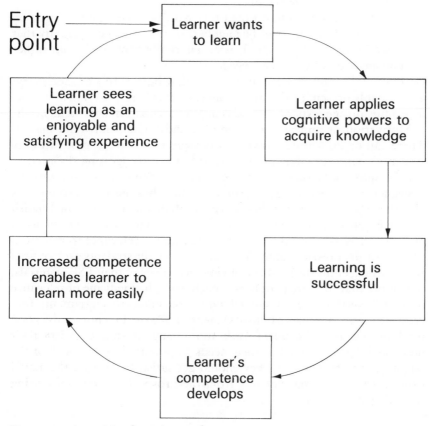

Figure 13: A positive learning cycle

The relationship between the cognitive and emotional aspects of learning is, therefore, one of vital importance to the success or otherwise of a language learning experience. This brings us to a matter which has been one of the most important elements in the development of ESP – motivation.

The most influential study of motivation in language learning has been Gardner and Lambert's (1972) study of bilingualism in French speaking Canada. They identified two forms of motivation: instrumental and integrative.

a) Instrumental motivation is the reflection of an external need. The learners are not learning a language because they want to (although this does not imply that they do not want to), but rather because they need to. The need may derive from varying sources: the need to sell things to speakers of the language; the need to pass an examination in the language; the need to read texts in the language for work or study. The need may vary, but the important factor is that the motivation is an external one.

b) Integrative motivation, on the other hand, derives from a desire on the part of the learners to be members of the speech community that uses a particular language. It is an internally generated *want* rather than an externally imposed *need*.

Gardner and Lambert's conclusion was that both forms of motivation are probably present in all learners but each exercises a varying influence, depending on age, experience and changing occupational or social needs.

Motivation, it appears, is a complex and highly individual matter. There can be no simple answers to the question: 'What motivates my students?' Unfortunately the ESP world, while recognising the need to ask this question, has apparently assumed that there is a simple answer: relevance to target needs. In practice this has been interpreted as meaning Medical texts for the student of Medicine, Engineering English for the Engineer and so on. But, as we shall see when we deal with needs analysis, there is more to motivation than simple relevance to perceived needs. For the present, suffice it to say that, if your students are not fired with burning enthusiasm by the obvious relevance of their ESP materials, remember that they are people not machines. The medicine of relevance may still need to be sweetened with the sugar of enjoyment, fun, creativity and a sense of achievement. ESP, as much as any good teaching, needs to be *intrinsically* motivating. It should satisfy their needs as learners as well as their needs as potential target users of the language. In other words, they should get satisfaction from the actual experience of learning, not just from the prospect of eventually using what they have learnt.

5   Learning and acquisition

Much debate has recently centred around the distinction made by Stephen Krashen (1981) between learning and acquisition. Learning is seen as a conscious process, while acquisition proceeds unconsciously. We have not in this section paid much attention to this distinction, using the two terms interchangeably. This reflects our view that for the second language learner both processes are likely to play a useful part and that a good ESP course will try to exploit both (see chapter 10).

6   A model for learning

In the light of the ideas we have discussed we will now present a model of the learning process, which will provide a practical source of reference for the ESP teacher and course designer.

First, picture the mind as a network of connections, rather like a road map (see figure 14). The individual houses, towns and villages represent items or bundles of knowledge. These various settlements, however, are only useful if they are connected to the main network by roads. The mind of the learner is like a development agency. It wants to bring the settlements into the network and so develop their potential. To achieve this, communication links must be established. But as with any communications network, links can only be established from existing links. In figure 14, for example, town X is unlikely to be connected into the network, unless towns Y and Z are already connected. The towns and villages in K can't be connected until some way is found of bridging the river. But, of course, once the river is bridged, it will open up a whole new area. The same applies to the settlements beyond the mountains. There is no limit to the number of links possible. Indeed the more links a place already has the more it is likely to attract. (See figure 14.)

Why have we pictured the mind as operating like this?

a) Individual items of knowledge, like the towns, have little significance on their own. They only acquire meaning and use when they are connected into the network of existing knowledge.

b) It is the existing network that makes it possible to construct new connections. So in the act of acquiring new knowledge it is the learner's existing knowledge that makes it possible to learn new items.

c) Items of knowledge are not of equal significance. Some items are harder to acquire, but may open up wide possibilities for further learning. Like a bridge across a river or a tunnel through a mountain, learning a generative rule may take time, but once it is there, it greatly increases the potential for further learning. This is why so often

49

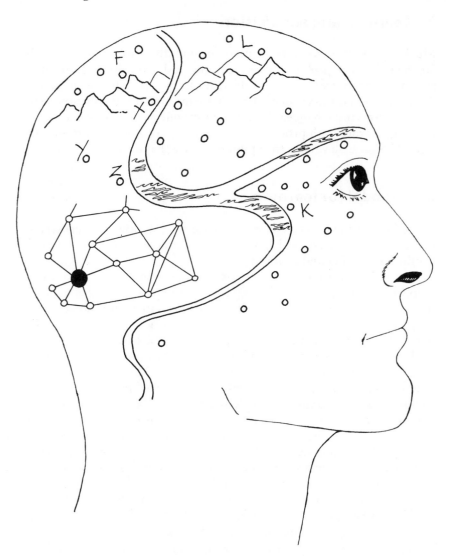

Figure 14: A model for learning

learning appears to progress in leaps and bounds. For a long time it might appear that little progress is being made; then suddenly the learner makes an enormous leap to a higher level of competence. Think of these leaps as the crossing of rivers, mountains and other major obstacles.

d) Roads and railways are not built haphazardly. They require planning. The roadbuilder has to recognise where problems lie and work out strategies for solving those problems. In the same way the learner will make better progress by developing strategies for solving the learning problems that will arise.

e) A communication network is a system. If the roadbuilder can see the whole system, the planning and construction of the roads will be a lot easier. Language is a system, too. If the learner sees it as just a haphazard set of arbitrary and capricious obstacles, learning will be difficult, if not impossible.

f) Last, but by no means least, before anyone builds a road, crosses a river or climbs a mountain, they must have some kind of motivation to do so. If they could not care less what is beyond the mountains, dislike the people who come from there or are simply afraid of travelling, the chances of communication links being established are minimal. First of all, there must be a need to establish the links. In ESP, this need is usually taken for granted. But, as anyone who has set out on a long and possibly difficult journey will know, a need is not enough. You can always find an excuse for not going. The traveller must also want to make the journey. And the traveller who can actually enjoy the challenges and the experiences of the journey, is more likely to want to repeat the activity. So, with learning, a need to acquire knowledge is a necessary factor, but of equal, if not greater importance, is the need to actually enjoy the process of acquisition.

Conclusion

In this chapter we have given a brief summary of the most important developments in approaches to learning and considered their relevance to ESP. In conclusion we should like to make two points:

a) We still do not know very much about learning. It is important, therefore, not to base any approach too narrowly on one theory. As with language descriptions, it is wise to take an eclectic approach, taking what is useful from each theory and trusting also in the evidence of your own experience as a teacher. It is probable that there are cognitive, affective and behaviourist aspects to learning, and each can be a resource to the ESP practitioner. For example, you may choose a behaviourist approach to the teaching of pronunciation, a cognitive approach to the teaching of grammar and use affective criteria in selecting your texts.

b) Theories of learning and language descriptions are not causally linked. As Corder (1973) says:

'There is no logical connection between a particular psychological theory of how grammar is learned and any particular theory of language structure...there is, however, an undoubted *historical* connection between them.'

Thus a behaviourist theory of learning does not have to accompany a structural view of language. Nor is there any causal link between a functional view of language and a cognitive learning theory. Indeed, it might be argued that structuralism with its emphasis on a finite set of rules lends itself more naturally to a cognitive approach, which stresses the importance of rules. A functional description, on the other hand, lacks a systematic grammar, so might be thought to fit better with a behaviourist view of learning (Hutchinson, 1984). In practice, the implication is that both language description and learning theory should be selected in accordance with Sweet's elegant principle of 'whether or not the learning of the language will be facilitated thereby' (quoted in Corder, 1973).

Having now considered the two main theoretical bases of course design, we shall look in the next chapter at the practical aspect that is often characterised as the distinguishing feature of ESP – needs analysis.

Tasks

1 Look at the rules of a behaviourist methodology on p. 40. In what ways do they conflict with the cognitive/affective views of learning?

2 What value do you think structural pattern drills have?

3 What is the importance to language teaching of the view of language behaviour as rule-governed activity?

4 Try to do the reading strategies tasks in figure 12.
   a) What strategies did you use to get your answers?
   b) How did you feel about the experience? Did you find it satisfying or frustrating?

5 One of the tasks in figure 12 comes from a 'general' component; the other is from a Science component.
   a) Which do you think is which? Why?
   b) Do you see any significant differences between them?

6 Consider the motivation of your own students. Does it resemble integrative or instrumental motivation?

7 What practical implications does the model of learning on p. 49 have for ESP materials and methodology? Make a set of precepts for a learning-centred methodology, like those for the behaviourist methodology.

6 Needs analysis

> From each according to his abilities, to each according to his needs.
>
> (Karl Marx)

We have defined ESP as an approach to course design which starts with the question 'Why do these learners need to learn English?' But it could be argued that this should be the starting question to any course, General or ESP. All courses are based on a perceived need of some sort. Otherwise why would English find its way on to a school or college timetable: someone at some time must have decided there was a need for it. What then, in the terms of our definition, is the difference between ESP and General English?

The answer to this very reasonable question is 'in theory nothing, in practice a great deal'. It is often argued that the needs of the General English learner, for example the schoolchild, are not specifiable. This is an assumption that owes more to institutional inertia and the weight of tradition than to any reality, but it is a powerful force nevertheless. In fact, this is the weakest of all arguments, because it is always possible to specify needs, even if it is only the need to pass the exam at the end of the school year. There is always an identifiable need of some sort.

What distinguishes ESP from General English is not the *existence* of a need as such but rather an *awareness* of the need. If learners, sponsors and teachers know why the learners need English, that awareness will have an influence on what will be acceptable as reasonable content in the language course and, on the positive side, what potential can be exploited. Thus, although it might appear on the surface that the ESP course is characterised by its content (Science, Medicine, Commerce, Tourism etc.), this is, in fact, only a secondary consequence of the primary matter of being able to readily specify why the learners need English. Put briefly, it is not so much the nature of the need which distinguishes the ESP from the General course but rather the awareness of a need.

This being said, we would still maintain that any course should be based on an analysis of learner need. This is one way in which ESP procedures can have a useful effect on General English and indicates once more the need for a common approach. The answers to the analysis will probably be different, but the questions that need to be asked are the same. Nevertheless, for the time being, the tradition persists in General English that learner needs can't be specified and as a result no attempt is usually made to discover learners' true needs. Thus if we had to state in practical terms the irreducible minimum of an ESP approach to course design, it would be needs analysis, since it is the awareness of a target situation – a definable need to communicate in English – that distinguishes the ESP learner from the learner of General English.

In chapters 4 and 5 we looked at some of the questions that should be asked about the nature of language and the teaching/learning process in general. In this chapter we shall look at the more specific matter of needs analysis. We shall be seeking answers to two questions. Firstly, what do we mean by 'needs'? Secondly, what kind of information should a needs analysis tell us?

Probably, the most thorough and widely known work on needs analysis is John Munby's *Communicative Syllabus Design* (1978). Munby presents a highly detailed set of procedures for discovering target situation needs. He calls this set of procedures the Communication Needs Processor (CNP). The CNP consists of a range of questions about key communication variables (topic, participants, medium etc.) which can be used to identify the target language needs of any group of learners.

The work marked a watershed in the development of ESP. With the development of the CNP it seemed as if ESP had come of age. The machinery for identifying the needs of any group of learners had been provided: all the course designer had to do was to operate it. However, *Communicative Syllabus Design* proved to be a watershed in quite another way. By taking the analysis of target needs to its logical conclusion, it showed the ultimate sterility of a language-centred approach to needs analysis. It illustrated, in effect, not how much could be learnt from a 'scientific' needs analysis, but rather how little. Why was this so?

The answer lies in the first of our questions about needs analysis: 'What do we mean by needs?' In the language-centred approach, the answer to this question would be 'the ability to comprehend and/or produce the linguistic features of the target situation', for example the ability to understand the passive voice. Thus what the CNP produces is a list of the linguistic features of the target situation. But there is much more to needs than this.

In the first instance, we can make a basic distinction between *target needs* (i.e. what the learner needs to do in the target situation) and *learning needs* (i.e. what the learner needs to do in order to learn). We shall consider *learning needs* later, but even within the category of *target needs* we can identify further divisions under the general heading of need.

1 What are target needs?

'Target needs' is something of an umbrella term, which in practice hides a number of important distinctions. It is more useful to look at the target situation in terms of *necessities*, *lacks* and *wants*.

a) *Necessities*

We can call 'necessities' the type of need determined by the demands of the target situation; that is, what the learner has to know in order to function effectively in the target situation. For example, a businessman or -woman might need to understand business letters, to communicate effectively at sales conferences, to get the necessary information from sales catalogues and so on. He or she will presumably also need to know the linguistic features – discoursal, functional, structural, lexical – which are commonly used in the situations identified. This information is relatively easy to gather. It is a matter of observing what situations the learner will need to function in and then analysing the constituent parts of them.

The following example of this procedure is adapted from Munby (1978), and it shows the necessities for a learner who works as a head waiter in a hotel:

Sample 'communication activities'	Related 'micro-functions'	Language forms (productive)
7. 1. 1 Attending to customers' arrival	7. 1. 1 1. intention 2. prohibit 3. direct etc.	I will bring the menu. I am afraid we are full/closed. Please follow me/Will you sit here please.
7. 1. 2 Attending to customers' order	7. 1. 2 1. suggestive 2. advise 3. describe etc.	May I suggest the ....? (etc.) May I recommend the ....? (etc.) You may find the .... too hot/spicy.
7. 1. 3 Serving the order, etc.	7. 1. 3 1. question	.... for you, sir/madam? The ....?

Figure 15: A needs analysis using the CNP

b) *Lacks*

To identify necessities alone, however, is not enough, since the concern in ESP is with the needs of particular learners. You also need to know what the learner knows already, so that you can then decide which of the necessities the learner lacks. One target situation necessity might be to read texts in a particular subject area. Whether or not the learners need instruction in doing this will depend on how well they can do it already. The target proficiency in other words, needs to be matched against the existing proficiency of the learners. The gap between the two can be referred to as the learner's lacks (Hutchinson, Waters and Breen 1979).

c) *Wants*

So far, we have considered target needs only in an objective sense, with the actual learners playing no active role. But the learners too, have a view as to what their needs are. As Richterich (1984 p. 29) comments:

'...a need does not exist independent of a person. It is people who build their images of their needs on the basis of data relating to themselves and their environment.'

We have stressed above that it is an awareness of need that characterises the ESP situation. But awareness is a matter of perception, and perception may vary according to one's standpoint. Learners may well have a clear idea of the 'necessities' of the target situation: they will certainly have a view as to their 'lacks'. But it is quite possible that the learners' views will conflict with the perceptions of other interested parties: course designers, sponsors, teachers. Some examples will illustrate this:

i) Karl Jensen is a German engineer who has a frequent and important need to read texts in English. He also needs to talk to overseas colleagues occasionally, for example, at the annual planning conference. The company he works for is a multi-national company and the operating language for communication outside national boundaries is English, although the majority of workers are non-native speakers. By any quantitative analysis Karl Jensen's need is for reading, because it is a much more frequent activity for him. But he feels a far stronger need to spend his time in the English class improving his oral competence. Why? The answer lies in the way in which he identifies his own personality with the use of a foreign language. He reads in private and at his own speed: he can use a dictionary, if he wants. But when he is speaking, his pride is on the line: his English competence (or lack of it, as he sees it) is exposed for all to see and he is under pressure to participate at a speed determined by the discourse. Therefore, Karl Jensen sees his greatest need as being the improvement of his oral proficiency.

ii) Li Yu Zhen is a Chinese graduate in Chemistry, who is going to study in the United States. She needs to be able to survive socially and professionally in an English-speaking community. Fluency is, therefore, her greatest need. Li Yu Zhen, however, prefers to spend her time improving her knowledge of English grammar. Why? Her answer lies in her own estimation of priorities. In order to be accepted for her course of study she must first pass a test. The most important criterion in the test is grammatical accuracy. Li Yu Zhen, therefore, sees her priority need as being to pass the test.

iii) José Lima is a Brazilian salesman. He needs to be able to talk on the telephone to customers and to other colleagues. He also needs to read catalogues and business letters. José is an outgoing, sociable man, who gets on easily with people. His spoken English is not very accurate, but is fluent. His employer feels that José's real need is for greater accuracy in spoken conversation, because it reflects badly on the company's image to have one of its representatives speaking very incorrect English. However, José feels that his spoken English is very good, and he resents the implication that it is not. After all, he communicates very well. He sees the English classes as a criticism of his performance as a salesman. He, therefore, has little motivation to attend classes.

As these case studies show, there is no necessary relationship between necessities as perceived by sponsor or ESP teacher and what the learners want or feel they need. (It is also quite likely that the views of sponsor and teacher will similarly be at odds!) Bearing in mind the importance of learner motivation in the learning process, learner perceived wants cannot be ignored. What this means in practical terms is well illustrated by Richard Mead's (1980) account of his research into the motivation of students following ESP courses in the faculties of Medicine, Agriculture and Veterinary Science at a university in the Middle East.

The students were all given ESP courses based on texts from their subject specialisms: Medical texts for the Medical students and so on. This, it was assumed, would motivate the students because of the apparent relevance to their course of study. When Mead enquired into the interest the students had in their specialisms, however, he discovered that only the Medical students were really motivated by their subject-specific texts. The Agriculture and Veterinary students were not motivated by their subject-specific texts, because they didn't really want to study those subjects. They had wanted to be medical doctors, but there were not enough places in the medical faculty to accommodate them all. They had opted for their specialisms as very poor second bests. Agricultural and Veterinary texts, therefore, were like salt in a wound. They had a de-motivating effect, because they reminded the students of their frustrated ambitions. We might represent the necessities, lacks and wants in Mead's analysis as in figure 16.

	OBJECTIVE (i.e. as perceived by course designers)	SUBJECTIVE (i.e. as perceived by learners)
NECESSITIES	The English needed for success in Agricultural or Veterinary Studies	To reluctantly cope with a 'second-best' situation
LACKS	(Presumably) areas of English needed for Agricultural or Veterinary Studies	Means of doing Medical Studies
WANTS	To succeed in Agricultural or Veterinary Studies	To undertake Medical Studies

Figure 16: Necessities, lacks and wants

It can be seen from this analysis that objective and subjective views of needs can, and do, conflict, with a consequent de-stabilising effect on motivation. What should the teacher do in such a situation? There can be no clear-cut answers. Each situation must be judged according to the particular circumstances. What is important is that the ESP course designer or teacher is aware of such differences and takes account of them in materials and methodology. There is little point in taking an ESP approach, which is based on the principle of learner involvement, and then ignoring the learners' wishes and views. As Davies and Currie (1971) put it:

'A method which frustrates the predictions of the learner is patently bad...Much of [the] satisfaction [of] learners will come when they feel that the hurdles they themselves have predicted have been cleared.' (our brackets)

2 Gathering information about target needs

It follows from the above account that the analysis of target needs involves far more than simply identifying the linguistic features of the target situation. There are a number of ways in which information can be gathered about needs. The most frequently used are:

questionnaires;
interviews;
observation;
data collection e.g. gathering texts;
informal consultations with sponsors, learners and others.

In view of the complexity of needs which we have seen, it is desirable to use more than one of these methods. The choice will obviously depend on the time and resources available. It is also important to remember that needs analysis is not a once-for-all activity. It should be a continuing process, in which the conclusions drawn are constantly checked and re-assessed (see e.g. Drobnic, 1978).

The analysis of target situation needs is in essence a matter of asking questions about the target situation and the attitudes towards that situation of the various participants in the learning process. Detailed procedures for gathering information are beyond the scope of this book. There are a number of books and articles that may be referred to for this purpose, for example Mackay (1978), Munby (1978), Cohen and Mannion (1980), Richterich and Chancerel (1980). The simple framework below outlines the kind of information that the course designer needs to gather from an analysis of target needs.

A target situation analysis framework

Why is the language needed?
- for study;
- for work;
- for training;
- for a combination of these;
- for some other purpose, e.g. status, examination, promotion.

How will the language be used?
- medium: speaking, writing, reading etc.;
- channel: e.g. telephone, face to face;
- types of text or discourse: e.g. academic texts, lectures, informal conversations, technical manuals, catalogues.

What will the content areas be?
- subjects: e.g. medicine, biology, architecture, shipping, commerce, engineering;
- level: e.g. technician, craftsman, postgraduate, secondary school.

Who will the learner use the language with?
- native speakers or non-native;
- level of knowledge of receiver: e.g. expert, layman, student;
- relationship: e.g. colleague, teacher, customer, superior, subordinate.

Where will the language be used?
- physical setting: e.g. office, lecture theatre, hotel, workshop, library;
- human context: e.g. alone, meetings, demonstrations, on telephone;
- linguistic context: e.g. in own country, abroad.

When will the language be used?
– concurrently with the ESP course or subsequently;
– frequently, seldom, in small amounts, in large chunks.

In view of what has been said earlier in this chapter about needs and wants, it is clear that interpretations of needs can vary according to the point of view of the particular respondent. ESP, like any educational matter, is concerned with people, and as such is subject to all the vagaries and foibles of human behaviour. For example, in analysing the needs of students, it would be normal practice to ask both the lecturers and the students about their English needs. There may be a tendency on the part of the lecturers to exaggerate the need for English, since English-medium instruction is often considered to have higher status. The lecturer, in other words, has a personal investment in giving the impression that the level of English needed is high. The students, on the other hand, may give a much lower indication of the need for English, because they know (or would prefer to believe) that it is not really necessary. They might consider their interests to lie in English for their future employment, for social purposes or even in not having English at all.

It is obviously necessary to obtain answers to the questions from a variety of sources, and then to try and negotiate (delicately) a satisfactory compromise. We shall deal with the matter of what you do with the information gathered by needs analysis in Section 3.

3 Learning needs

Till now we have considered needs only in terms of target situation needs. We have been considering the question: 'What knowledge and abilities will the learners require in order to be able to perform to the required degree of competence in the target situation?'. Using our analogy of the ESP course as a journey, what we have done so far is to consider the starting point (lacks) and the destination (necessities), although we have also seen that there might be some dispute as to what that destination should be (wants). What we have not considered yet is the route. How are we going to get from our starting point to the destination? This indicates another kind of need: learning needs.

To understand what is meant by learning needs, let us look a little more closely at what happens in the analysis of target situation needs.

In looking at the target situation, the ESP course designer is asking the question: 'What does the expert communicator need to know in order to function effectively in this situation?' This information may be recorded in terms of language items, skills, strategies, subject knowledge etc.

What the analysis cannot do, however, is show *how* the expert communicator *learnt* the language items, skills and strategies that he or she uses (Smith, 1984). Analysing what people do tells you little, if anything, about how they learnt to do it. Yet, the whole ESP process is concerned not with *knowing* or *doing*, but with *learning*. It is naive to base a course design simply on the target objectives, just as it is naive to think that a journey can be planned solely in terms of the starting point and the destination. The needs, potential and constraints of the route (i.e. the learning situation) must also be taken into account, if we are going to have any useful analysis of learner needs.

An example of what this means may be seen in the matter of choosing texts.

Let us say, we are preparing materials for a group of learners who need to read texts on Systems. Most of the available texts are long and dull. Should these texts be used for ESP? We would say no. The learners' motivation in the target situation will not necessarily carry over to the ESP classroom. They may well have to read very dull texts in their work or studies, but they probably have some strong motivation to do so. This does not imply that they will accept or learn from dull texts in ESP. It may be more appropriate to look for texts that are more interesting or humorous in order to generate the motivation needed to learn English (Hutchinson and Waters, 1983). An imaginative example of a focus on the learning situation is James B. Herbolich's box kite project (1979). Herbolich describes a scheme in which Engineering students at the University of Kuwait had to build a box kite and write a manual explaining how to construct it. Herbolich gives five reasons for choosing the box kite as the object of the project:

'The mechanism should be (1) relatively new to the students; (2) related to a field of Engineering; (3) a device which allowed the attainment of new lexis; (4) a device which actually would operate; and (5) enjoyable to construct and test.'

It is interesting to consider how far the activity reflects target situation needs and how far the needs of the learning situation. The students would have to write manuals in the target situation and this obviously explains the choice of this particular mode of expression. The students were studying Engineering, hence reason (2) above. But this is the limit of the influence of the target situation. All the other reasons given derive from the needs of the learning situation – the need for a task that is enjoyable, fulfilling, manageable, generative etc. The project, in effect, is guided in terms of its general orientation by the target situation, but its specific content is a response to learning needs.

Herbolich's project reminds us once more that ESP learners are people. They may be learning about machines, but they are not the word-crunching machines which too many approaches to ESP seem to imply.

In the target situation they may need, for example, to read long, dull or complex texts, but their motivation to do so may be high because:
- they like the subject in general;
- examinations are looming;
- job/promotion prospects may be involved;
- they may be going on to do very interesting experiments or practical work based on the texts;
- they may like and/or respect the subject teacher or boss;
- they may be very good at their subject, but poor at English.

For all manner of possible reasons learners may be well motivated in the subject lesson or in their work, but totally turned off by encountering the same material in an ESP classroom. The target situation, in other words, is not a reliable indicator of what is needed or useful in the ESP learning situation. The target situation analysis can determine the destination; it can also act as a compass on the journey to give general direction, but we must choose our route according to the vehicles and guides available (i.e. the conditions of the learning situation), the existing roads within the learner's mind (i.e. their knowledge, skills and strategies) and the learners' motivation for travelling.

4 Analysing learning needs

To analyse learning needs, we can use a similar checklist to that used for target situation analysis:

A framework for analysing learning needs

Why are the learners taking the course?
- compulsory or optional;
- apparent need or not;
- Are status, money, promotion involved?
- What do learners think they will achieve?
- What is their attitude towards the ESP course? Do they want to improve their English or do they resent the time they have to spend on it?

How do the learners learn?
- What is their learning background?
- What is their concept of teaching and learning?
- What methodology will appeal to them?
- What sort of techniques are likely to bore/alienate them?

What resources are available?
– number and professional competence of teachers;
– attitude of teachers to ESP;
– teachers' knowledge of and attitude to the subject content;
– materials;
– aids;
– opportunities for out-of-class activities.

Who are the learners?
– age/sex/nationality;
– What do they know already about English?
– What subject knowledge do they have?
– What are their interests?
– What is their socio-cultural background?
– What teaching styles are they used to?
– What is their attitude to English or to the cultures of the English-speaking world?

Where will the ESP course take place?
– are the surroundings pleasant, dull, noisy, cold etc?

When will the ESP course take place?
– time of day;
– every day/once a week;
– full-time/part-time;
– concurrent with need or pre-need.

Conclusion

In this chapter we have looked at the most characteristic feature of ESP course design – needs analysis. We have tried to show that it is a complex process, involving much more than simply looking at what the learners will have to do in the target situation. Most of all, we have tried to stress that both target situation needs and learning needs must be taken into account. Analysis of target situation needs is concerned with language *use*. But language *use* is only part of the story. We also need to know about language *learning*. Analysis of the target situation can tell us what people *do* with language. What we also need to know is how people *learn* to do what they do with language. We need, in other words, a learning-centred approach to needs analysis.

Tasks

1 In what ways will an awareness of need affect an ESP course?

2 How might you analyse the needs of secondary school learners? What results do you think you would get?

3 What would you do faced with Mead's situation?

4 Make an analysis of your own learners' needs using the *Framework for analysing target needs*.

5 Analyse your own teaching/learning situation using the *Framework for analysing learning needs*.

6 Study your own ESP textbook or materials. Try to reconstruct the results of the needs analysis it is based on.

7 Approaches to course design

They must have the defects of their qualities.

(translated from Honoré de Balzac: *Le Lys dans la Vallée*)

Course design is the process by which the raw data about a learning need is interpreted in order to produce an integrated series of teaching-learning experiences, whose ultimate aim is to lead the learners to a particular state of knowledge. In practical terms this entails the use of the theoretical and empirical information available to produce a syllabus, to select, adapt or write materials in accordance with the syllabus, to develop a methodology for teaching those materials and to establish evaluation procedures by which progress towards the specified goals will be measured.

So let us assume we have completed our needs analysis and reviewed the theoretical models of learning and language available. We now have to face that crushing question: What do we do with the information we have gathered? Asking questions about learner needs will not of itself design a course. The data must be interpreted. We have got a lot of answers. But when we come to designing our course, we will find yet another series of questions. The data from our needs analysis can help to answer these questions. But care is needed: there is no necessary one-to-one transfer from needs analysis to course design. We have seen already that answers from one area (what learners need) and another (what learners want) may conflict. We must remember that there are external constraints (classroom facilities/time) that will restrict what is possible. There are also our own theoretical views and (not to be discounted) experience of the classroom to take into account.

There are probably as many different approaches to ESP course design as there are course designers. We can, however, identify three main types: language-centred, skills-centred and learning-centred.

1 Language-centred course design

This is the simplest kind of course design process and is probably the one most familiar to English teachers. It is particularly prevalent in ESP.

The language-centred course design process aims to draw as direct

65

a connection as possible between the analysis of the target situation and the content of the ESP course. It proceeds as follows:

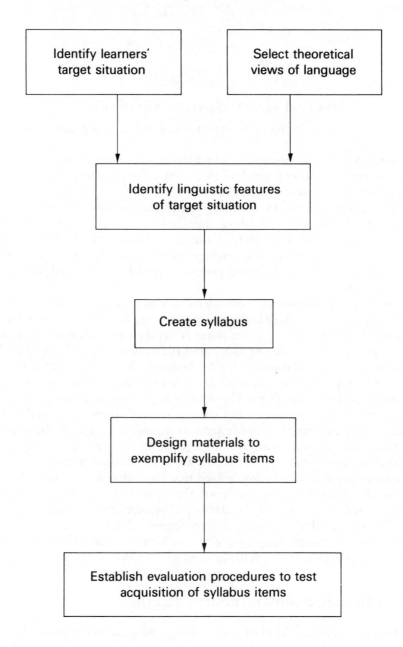

Figure 17: A language-centred approach to course design

At first sight, this may seem to be a very logical procedure. It starts with the learner, proceeds through various stages of analysis to a syllabus, thence to materials in use in the classroom and finally to evaluation of mastery of the syllabus items. However, logical and straightforward as it may seem, it has a number of weaknesses:

a) It starts from the learners and their needs, and thus it might be considered a learner-centred approach, but it is, in fact, not learner-centred in any meaningful sense of the term. The learner is simply used as a means of identifying the target situation. Instead of taking the whole of English and teaching it to the learner, as happens in General English, only a restricted area of the language is taught. As figure 18 shows, the learner is used solely as a way of locating the restricted area. Thereafter the learner plays no further part in the process. As we have seen, however, when considering needs analysis, the learner should be considered at every stage of the process. Yet, in this model the learning needs of the students are not accounted for at all. It is, therefore, not learner-centred, but simply learner-restricted.

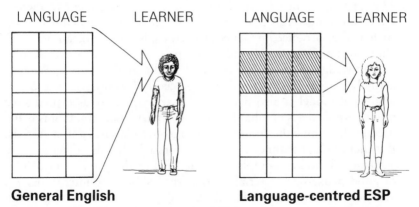

LANGUAGE　　　LEARNER　　　LANGUAGE　　　LEARNER

General English　　　　　**Language-centred ESP**

Figure 18: The learner-restricted syllabus

b) The language-centred process can also be criticised for being a static and inflexible procedure, which can take little account of the conflicts and contradictions that are inherent in any human endeavour. Once the initial analysis of the target situation is done, the course designer is locked into a relentless process. But what if the initial analysis is wrong? What if some crucial element, such as the unexpected motivational attitude of Mead's students (see above p. 57) is not taken into account? Any procedure must have flexibility, feedback channels and error tolerance built in so that it can respond to unsuspected or developing influences.

c) One of the alluring features of this model is that it appears to be systematic. But in so doing it engenders the false belief that learning itself is systematic – that the systematic analysis and presentation of language data will produce systematic learning in the learner. Unfortunately the role of systematisation in learning is not so simple. Certainly, there is a lot of evidence to show that the systematisation of knowledge plays a crucial role in the learning process: we learn by fitting individual items of knowledge together to create a meaningful predictive system. But the most important point here is that it must be an internally-generated system not an externally-imposed system. The fact that knowledge has been systematically analysed and systematically presented does not in any way imply that it will be systematically learnt. Learners have to make the system meaningful to themselves. And unfortunately we have to admit that we do not know enough about how the mind actually goes about creating its internal system of knowledge. We must, however, avoid the mistake made by the Audiolingual Approach of believing that because language has a describable system, describing that system will induce systematic learning.

d) The language-centred model gives no acknowledgement to factors which must inevitably play a part in the creation of any course. Data such as that produced by a needs analysis, is not important in itself. Data must be interpreted, and in interpreting we make use of all sorts of knowledge that are not revealed in the analysis itself. What is actually happening in the language-centred approach is that an analytical model is also being used inappropriately as a predictive model. An analysis of what happens in a particular situation is being used to determine the content of pedagogic syllabuses and materials. But there are all manner of other factors which will influence these activities. To take a simple example, one of the primary principles of good pedagogic materials is that they should be interesting. An analysis of language items cannot tell you whether a text or an activity is interesting. Thus, if materials are based on the language-centred model, then, either there are other factors being used, which are not acknowledged in the model, or, and sadly this is what seems so often to be the case, these learning factors are not considered to be important at all. As a teacher once remarked at a seminar on materials writing, 'It doesn't matter if it's boring. It's ESP.'

e) The language-centred analysis of target situation data is only at the surface level. It reveals very little about the competence that underlies the performance.

In summary, then, the logical, straightforward appeal of the language-centred approach is, in effect, its weakness. It fails to recognise the fact that, learners being people, learning is not a straightforward, logical process.

2 Skills-centred course design

The skills-centred approach to ESP has been widely applied in a number of countries, particularly in Latin America. Students in universities and colleges there have the limited, but important need to read subject texts in English, because they are unavailable in the mother tongue. In response to this need, a number of ESP projects have been set up with the specific aim of developing the students' ability to read in English (see above p. 13). The skills-centred approach is founded on two fundamental principles, one theoretical, the other pragmatic:

a) The basic theoretical hypothesis is that underlying any language behaviour are certain skills and strategies, which the learner uses in order to produce or comprehend discourse. A skills-centred approach aims to get away from the surface performance data and look at the competence that underlies the performance (see 1(e) above). A skills-centred course, therefore, will present its learning objectives (though probably not explicitly) in terms of both performance and competence. This example from a Brazilian ESP syllabus for Library Science students is given in Maciel et al. (1983) (our brackets):

> *General objective* (i.e. performance level):
> The student will be able to catalogue books written in English.
> *Specific objectives* (i.e. competence level):
> The student will be able to:
> –extract the gist of a text by skimming through it.
> –extract relevant information from the main parts of a book.

b) The pragmatic basis for the skills-centred approach derives from a distinction made by Widdowson (1981) between goal-oriented courses and process-oriented courses. Holmes (1982) points out that:*

> 'In ESP the main problem is usually one of time available and student experience. First, the aims may be defined in terms of what is *desirable*, – i.e. to be able to read in the literature of the students' specialism, but there may be nowhere near enough time to reach this aim during the period of the course. Secondly, the students may be in their first year of studies with little experience of the literature of their specialism...Accordingly both these factors...may be constraints which say right from the start, "The aims cannot be achieved *during* the course."'

Holmes puts his finger on a contradiction that arises from interpreting 'needs' in the narrow sense of 'target situation necessities'. If the ESP course is designed in terms of goals, there is in effect a tacit admission that a large number of students will fail the course. Since ESP is by

---

* Our use of the term 'skills-centred' can be taken as synonymous with Widdowson's (and Holmes') 'process-oriented'.

its very nature a process that is intended to enable people to achieve a purpose, it is at best a little odd to frame the course in such a way as to almost predict failure. The process-oriented approach tries to avoid this problem by removing the distinction between the ESP course and the target situation. The ESP course is not seen as a self-sufficient unit from which learners emerge as proficient target situation performers, because, as Holmes points out, a number of students are unlikely to achieve this proficiency. Instead, the ESP course and the target situation are seen as a continuum of constantly developing degrees of proficiency with no cut-off point of success or failure. The emphasis in the ESP course, then, is not on achieving a particular set of goals, but on enabling the learners to achieve what they can within the given constraints:

'The process-oriented approach...is at least realistic in concentrating on strategies and processes of making students aware of their own abilities and potential, and motivating them to tackle target texts on their own after the end of the course, so that they can continue to improve.' (ibid.)

The skills-centred model, therefore, is a reaction both to the idea of specific registers of English as a basis for ESP and to the practical constraints on learning imposed by limited time and resources. In essence it sees the ESP course as helping learners to develop skills and strategies which will continue to develop *after* the ESP course itself. Its aim is not to provide a specified corpus of linguistic knowledge but to make the learners into better processors of information. We might present the skills-centred model as in figure 19.

The role of needs analysis in a skills-centred approach is twofold. Firstly, it provides a basis for discovering the underlying competence that enables people to perform in the target situation. Secondly, it enables the course designer to discover the potential knowledge and abilities that the learners bring to the ESP classroom.

The skills-centred approach, therefore, can certainly claim to take the learner more into account than the language-centred approach:
a) It views language in terms of how the mind of the learner processes it rather than as an entity in itself.
b) It tries to build on the positive factors that the learners bring to the course, rather than just on the negative idea of 'lacks'.
c) It frames its objectives in open-ended terms, so enabling learners to achieve at least something.
Yet, in spite of its concern for the learner, the skills-centred approach still approaches the learner as a *user* of language rather than as a *learner* of language. The processes it is concerned with are the processes of language *use* not of language *learning*. It is with this distinction in mind that we turn to the third approach to course design.

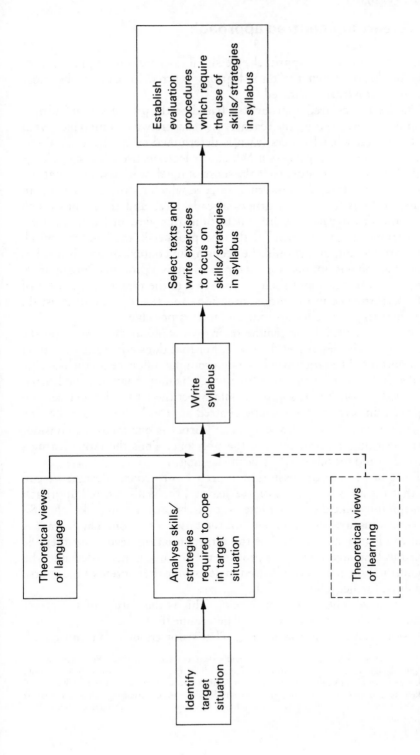

Figure 19: A skills-centred approach to course design

3 A learning-centred approach

Before describing this approach, we should expand our explanation of why we have chosen the term learn*ing*-centred instead of the more common term learn*er*-centred.

The learner-centred approach* is based on the principle that learning is totally determined by the learner. As teachers we can influence what we teach, but what learners learn is determined by the learners alone. Learning is seen as a process in which the learners use what knowledge or skills they have in order to make sense of the flow of new information. Learning, therefore, is an internal process, which is crucially dependent upon the knowledge the learners already have and their ability and motivation to use it. It is difficult to fault this view of learning, if we see learning simply in terms of the end product in the learner's mind. But learning can, and should, be seen in the context in which it takes place. Learning is not just a mental process, it is a process of negotiation between individuals and society. Society sets the target (in the case of ESP, performance in the target situation) and the individuals must do their best to get as close to that target as is possible (or reject it). The learners will certainly determine their own route to the target and the speed at which they travel the route, but that does not make the target unimportant. The target still has a determining influence on the possible routes. In the learning process, then, there is more than just the learner to consider. For this reason we would reject the term a learner-centred approach in favour of a learning-centred approach to indicate that the concern is to maximise learning. The learner is one factor to consider in the learning process, but not the only one. Thus the term: learner-centred would for our purpose be misleading.

To return to our discussion of approaches to course design, we can see that for all its emphasis on the learner, the skills-centred approach does not fully take the learner into account, because it still makes the ESP learning situation too dependent on the target situation. The learner is used to identify and to analyse the target situation needs. But then, as with the language-centred approach, the learner is discarded and the target situation analysis is allowed to determine the content of the course with little further reference to the learner.

A language-centred approach says: This is the nature of the target situation performance and that will determine the ESP course.

A skills-centred approach says: That's not enough. We must look

---

* A truly learner-centred approach does not really exist at the current time. We would not like to give the impression that it is a formalised approach in actual use. Indeed since most learning takes place within institutionalised systems, it is difficult to see how such an approach could be taken, as it more or less rules out pre-determined syllabuses, materials etc. Thus it should be viewed more as a theoretical attack on established procedure than as a practical approach to course design.

behind the target performance data to discover what processes enable someone to perform. Those processes will determine the ESP course.

A learning-centred approach says: That's not enough either. We must look beyond the competence that enables someone to perform, because what we really want to discover is not the competence itself, but how someone acquires that competence.

We might see the relationship in this diagram:

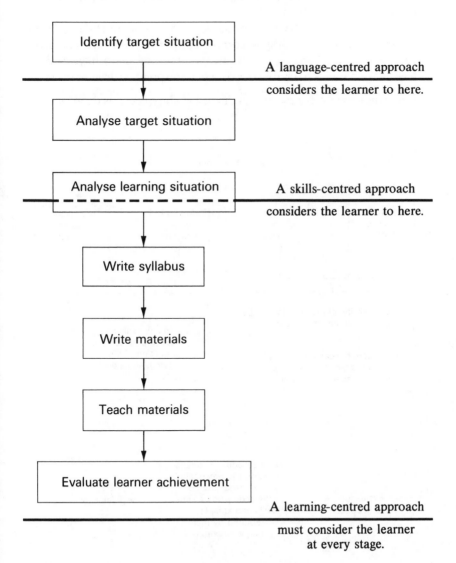

Figure 20: A comparison of approaches to course design

Course design

Figure 20 shows that a learning-centred approach to course design takes account of the learner at every stage of the design process. This has two implications:

a) Course design is a negotiated process. There is no single factor which has an outright determining influence on the content of the course. The ESP learning situation and the target situation will both influence the nature of the syllabus, materials, methodology and evaluation procedures. Similarly each of these components will influence and be influenced by the others.

b) Course design is a dynamic process. It does not move in a linear fashion from initial analysis to completed course. Needs and resources vary with time. The course design, therefore, needs to have built-in feedback channels to enable the course to respond to developments.

The learning-centred course design process is shown in this diagram:

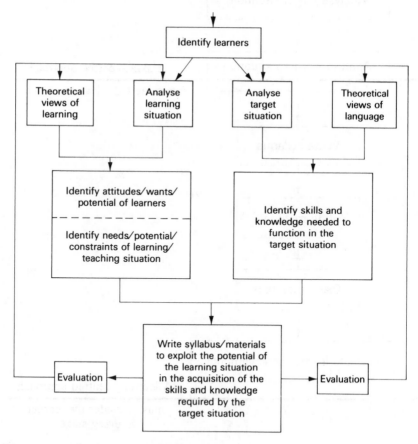

Figure 21: A learning-centred approach to course design

What does it mean in practical terms to take a learning-centred approach to ESP? We will look in more detail at this question in *Materials design* (chapter 10). For the moment let us look at a fairly common example at the level of course design.

A needs analysis reveals that the ESP learners need English in order to be able to read texts in their subject specialism. They have no need to write, speak or listen to English. Their sole need is to read English texts. If we followed a language-centred or skills-centred approach to course design, we might conclude that ESP lessons would concern themselves only with the activity of reading texts. There would be no listening work; all discussion would be in the native language and writing tasks would be minimal. This would be a logical application of the models for course design above (figures 18 and 19). But if we took a learning-centred approach, we would need to ask further questions and consider other factors, before determining the content and methodology of the course.

a) Can we only learn to read effectively by reading or can the other skills help the learners to become better readers? For example, is it possible that learners might grasp the structure of texts more easily by writing texts themselves? Can a knowledge of the sound or rhythm of a language help in reading? Stevick (1982) stresses the importance for memory of creating rich images in a way which closely parallels our own model of learning as a network-building process (see chapter 4):

> 'The higher the quality of the image – that is, the richer and better integrated it is – the more easily we will be able to get back one part of it when we encounter another part.'

We can apply this argument to the question of skills. If an image gets into the brain through a number of different pathways – by hearing, reading, writing and speaking – that image is likely to be a richer image than if it gets in through only one pathway. The image will thereby be much stronger and much more easily accessible, since it will have more connections into the network. The fact that the learner will eventually use the knowledge gained only for reading is largely irrelevant. What is of most concern is how the learner can learn that knowledge most effectively. If the effectiveness of the process can be enriched by the use of other skills, then that is what should be done.

b) What are the implications for methodology of having a mono-skill focus? Will it lead to a lack of variety in lessons or a limited range of exercise types, which will soon induce boredom in the learners? Could other skills be used to increase variety? These are not trivial questions. One of the basic paradoxes of language teaching is that we need to repeat things in order to learn them, but frequent repetition creates boredom: our minds switch off and learning is

75

minimal. Variety is, therefore, not just a nice thing to have for its own sake: it is a vital element in keeping the learners' minds alert and focussed on the task in hand. Processing the same information through a variety of skills is one way of achieving reinforcement while still maintaining concentration. It is much more difficult to get variety if we have to operate to target situation imposed constraints, such as a restriction to one skill (see chapter 11, *Methodology*).

c) How will the students react to doing tasks involving other skills? Will they appreciate the greater variety and interest of the activities or will they say 'I don't need to understand spoken English, so why are you asking me to listen to something in English? I need to read.'

d) Do the resources in the classroom allow the use of other skills? Is it quiet enough to do listening or speaking work? Can the teacher handle an integrated skills approach?

e) How will the learners react to discussing things in the mother tongue? Will it help them to feel more secure? Will it enable them to express their views more easily and freely. Or will they feel that it isn't really helping them to learn English?

f) How will the learners' attitudes vary through the course? At first they may prefer a reading only approach, because it is novel and may give them a good sense of achievement. Will this motivation carry on through the whole course, however? Will the learners get bored with the same kinds of activities and start to want a more varied methodology?

g) How do the learners feel about reading as an activity? Is it something they like doing, or is it an activity that they avoid where possible, even in the mother tongue? If the latter is the case, will a reading only approach help to remove some of their aversion to reading or will it reinforce existing antipathies?

The answers to the questions we have been considering might reinforce the idea of doing reading only or they might indicate that an integrated skills approach is required. The answers will vary depending on the learners and the learning context. The example, however, serves to show how factors concerned with learning may affect the design of a course, sometimes in total contradiction to the apparent needs of the target situation. The *Framework for analysing learning needs* (see above p. 62) provides more questions that could be asked. The answers, as we have said, will vary according to the individual situation and may vary within the timespan of the course. The important point is that these questions must be asked and the results allowed to influence the course design.

Conclusion

In this chapter we have looked at the question of how the data of a needs analysis can be used to design an effective ESP course. Traditionally the target situation analysis has had a direct determining influence on the development of syllabus, materials, methodology and tests. We have argued that the course design process should be much more dynamic and interactive. In particular, factors concerned with learning must be brought into play at all stages of the design process. We have called this a learning-centred approach – an approach with the avowed aim of maximising the potential of the learning situation. Such an approach is inevitably more complex: it is based, after all, on a recognition of the complexity of the learning process. But everything must have the defects of its qualities. In the next section we shall look at how the approach can be applied to the construction of a syllabus and to the evaluation, design and teaching of materials.

Tasks

1 Analyse an ESP course in your institution and decide what approach has been used to design it. What do you feel are the merits and drawbacks of the design?

2 What do you think a fully learner-centred course would be like?

3 The Malaysian and the Brazilian ESP Projects (see above p. 13) differ in their attitude to skills. The University of Malaya project has a Spoken Interaction component (Chitravelu, 1980), while the Brazilian project uses the mother tongue for all oral work:
   a) What factors might have influenced the course designers in these two projects in making their decisions?
   b) Consider the 'reading only' problem in your own situation. What answers do you think you would get to the questions we raise above (p. 75)?

4 A learning-centred approach to course design is complex and time-consuming. Do you think it is worth the trouble?

Section 3   Application

By their fruits ye shall know them.

(Gospel of St. Matthew 7:20)

In the first two sections of this book, we have looked at the principles and practices that lie behind ESP course design. In this section we will be concerned with the detailed implementation of the design into a syllabus, materials, a methodology and evaluation procedures. First a word of caution. Books and courses must proceed in a linear fashion: one page must follow another; one lesson must follow another. Knowledge has to be segmented for presentation somehow. But this does not carry any implications for importance or procedure. In dealing with the syllabus before materials writing, we are not suggesting that the syllabus is more important than the materials, nor that the syllabus must be written before the materials. Indeed it would be perfectly possible to deal with them the other way around, just as it is perfectly possible to write the materials before the syllabus. The teaching/learning process is a complex and dynamic process, with all the various factors influencing each other (see figure 21 p. 74).

8 The syllabus

I must Create a System, or be enslaved by another Man's.

(William Blake, 'Jerusalem')

In this first chapter on the applications of a course design model, we shall be looking at the syllabus and considering the following questions:
1 What do we mean by a syllabus?
2 Why should we have a syllabus?
3 On what criteria can a syllabus be organised?
4 What role should a syllabus play in the course design process?

1 What do we mean by a syllabus?

Most teachers might regard this as an unnecessary question. A syllabus is a document which says what will (or at least what should) be learnt. But, in fact, there are several different ways in which a syllabus can be defined. This stems from the fact that the statement of what will be learnt passes through several different stages before it reaches its destination in the mind of the learner. Each stage on its route imposes a further layer of interpretation.

a) The evaluation syllabus

As we have said, at its simplest level a syllabus can be described as a statement of what is to be learnt. This kind of syllabus will be most familiar as the document that is handed down by ministries or other regulating bodies. It states what the successful learner will know by the end of the course. In effect, it puts on record the basis on which success or failure will be evaluated. Thus we might refer to this as an *evaluation* syllabus. It reflects an official assumption as to the nature of language and linguistic performance. For example, if the syllabus is framed in terms of grammatical structures, this reflects a view that knowing a language consists of knowing the constituent structures. It would be impossible to produce an evaluation syllabus without having a view of what language is and thus how it can be broken down.

b) The organisational syllabus

As well as listing what should be learnt, a syllabus can also state the order in which it is to be learnt. We might call this an *organisational* syllabus. In a rough sense, evaluation syllabuses fulfil this role, in that they normally list what should be learnt in, for example, the first year of learning etc. The organisational syllabus is most familiar in the form of the contents page of a textbook, and it is this form of syllabus that most people would think of when asked: 'What is a syllabus?' The organisational syllabus differs from the evaluation syllabus in that it carries assumptions about the nature of learning as well as language, since, in organising the items in a syllabus, it is necessary to consider factors which depend upon a view of how people learn, e.g.:
– What is more easily learnt?
– What is more fundamental to learning?
– Are some items needed in order to learn other items?
– What is more useful in the classroom?
Criteria like these must be used in order to determine the order of items. The organisational syllabus, therefore, is an implicit statement about the nature of language and of learning.

c) The materials syllabus

The two syllabuses considered so far might be regarded as pure syllabuses, in that they have not been interpreted. They are a straightforward statement of what is to be learnt with some indication of the order in which the items should be learnt. The syllabuses say nothing about how learning will be achieved. But a syllabus, like a course design model, is only as good as the interpretation that is put on it. On its route to the learner the organisational syllabus goes through a series of interpretations.

The first person to interpret the syllabus is usually the materials writer. So we get our third kind of syllabus – the *materials* syllabus. In writing materials, the author adds yet more assumptions about the nature of language, language learning and language use. The author decides the contexts in which the language will appear, the relative weightings and integration of skills, the number and type of exercises to be spent on any aspect of language, the degree of recycling or revision. These can all have their effect on whether and how well something is learnt. For example, if certain vocabulary items are presented in texts which appeal to the learners, they are more likely to be remembered, because the learners' attention will be more involved.

d) The teacher syllabus

The second stage of interpretation usually comes through the teacher. The great majority of students in the world learn language through the mediation of a teacher. Thus we have the *teacher* syllabus (Breen, 1984). Like the materials writer, the teacher can influence the clarity, intensity and frequency of any item, and thereby affect the image that the learners receive. Stevick (1984) recounts how an inexperienced teacher would finish in two minutes an activity that he would spend twenty minutes on. This kind of variability will inevitably affect the degree of learning.

e) The classroom syllabus

As every teacher knows, what is planned and what actually happens in a lesson are two different things (Allwright, 1984b). A lesson is a communicative event, which is created by the interaction of a number of forces. We might use our analogy of a journey again to illustrate this point. The lesson plan is like the planned route, but like a planned route it can be affected by all sorts of conditions along the way – the unexpected traffic jam, the slow-moving vehicle that you get stuck behind, the diversion because of road works, the new one-way system that you get lost in. But the journey might also be helped along by the new stretch of motorway, the company of travelling companions, fine weather etc. The classroom, too, creates conditions which will affect the nature of a planned lesson. These might be extraneous factors, such as noise from outside, hot weather, interruptions to deal with an administrative matter, a visitor. They might come from the learners as a group: perhaps they are tired after a long day, excitable after an incident in the break. Individual students might hold matters up by asking questions or distracting the attention of the class. They might on the other hand make a lesson memorable by putting an interesting question or telling an amusing anecdote.

The classroom, then, is not simply a neutral channel for the passage of information from teacher to learner. It is a dynamic, interactive environment, which affects the nature both of what is taught and what is learnt. The classroom thus generates its own syllabus (Breen, 1984).

f) The learner syllabus

The syllabuses we have considered till now might all be referred to as external syllabuses. The learners might participate in their creation to some extent, but essentially they are external to the learner. The last type of syllabus, however, is an internal syllabus. It is the network of knowledge that develops in the learner's brain and which enables that learner to comprehend and store the later knowledge. We might call this the *learner* syllabus (Breen, 1984).

The learner syllabus differs from all the other types we have mentioned not just in being internal as opposed to external, but in that it faces in the opposite direction. It is a retrospective record of what has been learnt rather than a prospective plan of what will be learnt (Candlin, 1984). The importance of the learner syllabus lies in the fact that it is through the filter of this syllabus that the learner views the other syllabuses. What is in that learner syllabus, in other words, will have a crucial influence on whether and how future knowledge is learnt. It is for this reason that the learners must be taken into account on a continuing basis through every stage of the course design process (see above figure 21).

There is, then, not just one syllabus, but several, and the teaching-learning process involves the interaction of them all. When we use the term 'syllabus', we should be very clear which one we are referring to. In particular, do we mean the external specification of future learning or the internal construct developed by the learner? But the most important point of all to draw from this analysis is that there is no necessary relationship between any of the syllabuses, and in particular, *there is no direct relationship between the starting point of the evaluation syllabus and the end point of the learner syllabus* (see Allwright, 1984b). On any empirical evidence, this should be blindingly obvious and yet the fallacy persists: 'I have taught the syllabus. Therefore the students have learnt what is in the syllabus.'

2 Why should we have a syllabus*?

In view of the amount of work that goes into syllabus design and the considerable weight of authority that syllabuses have, we might usefully consider whether they are necessary. This will reveal that just as there are acknowledged and hidden syllabuses, there are also acknowledged and hidden reasons for having a syllabus.

a) Language is a complex entity. It cannot be learnt in one go. We have to have some way of breaking down the complex into manageable units. The syllabus, in defining the constituent parts of language knowledge, thus provides a practical basis for the division of assessment, textbooks and learning time.

b) In addition to its practical benefits, a syllabus also gives moral support to the teacher and learner, in that it makes the language learning task appear manageable.

---

* In questions 2–4 we shall use the word syllabus in the sense of the evaluation/organisational syllabus.

c) A syllabus, particularly an ESP syllabus, also has a cosmetic role. Sponsors and students will want some reassurance that their investment of money and/or time will be worthwhile. If nothing else, the syllabus shows that some thought and planning has gone into the development of a course. This aspect is, obviously, of particular importance when there are commercial sponsors involved.

d) Returning to our analogy of learning as a journey, the syllabus can be seen as a statement of projected routes, so that teacher and learner not only have an idea of where they are going, but how they might get there.

e) A syllabus is an implicit statement of views on the nature of language and learning. A syllabus will normally be expressed in terms of what is taken to be the most important aspect of language learning. If we lay out a syllabus in structural terms, we are saying that knowledge of the structures of the language constitutes the most important element of language competence. If we take a skills basis, we are saying that skills are the most important aspect and so on. A syllabus, then, tells the teacher and the student not only *what* is to be learnt, but, implicitly, *why* it is to be learnt.

f) A syllabus provides a set of criteria for materials selection and/or writing. It defines the kind of texts to look for or produce, the items to focus on in exercises etc. This is probably one of the commonest uses for a syllabus, but it can be one of the most damaging to the course design, if wrongly used (see 4 below p. 90).

g) Uniformity is a necessary condition of any institutionalised activity, such as education. It is deemed to be important that standards within a system are as equal as possible. A syllabus is one way in which standardisation is achieved (or at least attempted).

h) In that teaching is intended to lead a learner to a particular state of knowledge, there need to be criteria against which success or failure in reaching that state will be assessed. A syllabus, therefore, provides a visible basis for testing.

It is clear from this list of roles that a syllabus is an important document in the teaching/learning process. Indeed, its importance probably stems from its multi-functional purpose. But therein also lie the dangers:

a) We should be aware of why we want a syllabus and what we will use it for. If it is really just for cosmetic purposes to placate a sponsor, then we should not try to use it as a means of selecting texts or deciding what to put in the exercises.

b) A syllabus is a model – a statement of an ideal. A syllabus is not, therefore, a statement of what will be learnt. It is important to remember that a syllabus can only constitute an approximate statement of what will be *taught* (though, even here the divergence may be considerable). It can predict very little about what will be *learnt*. A syllabus can never be more than a statement of a teaching ideal.

c) Syllabuses cannot express the intangible factors that are so crucial to learning: emotions, personalities, subjective views, motivation.

d) Syllabuses cannot take account of individual differences. Just as they are a statement of the ideal in language terms, they also implicitly define the ideal learner.

The role of the syllabus is a complex one, but it clearly satisfies a lot of needs. We need crucially to be aware of the different roles that the syllabus plays, so that it can be used most appropriately. In particular we need to recognise its ideal nature and, therefore, its limitations as an indicator of learning.

3 On what criteria can a syllabus be organised?

We noted above that one of the main purposes of a syllabus is to break down the mass of knowledge to be learnt into manageable units. This breakdown (unless it is to be completely random) has to be based on certain criteria. Presented below are some contents lists from a range of ESP courses, illustrating the different criteria that can be used.

a) *Topic syllabus*

1 The Rig
2 Fishing Jobs
3 Traps and Geology
4 Reservoir Fluids
5 Natural Flow
6 Blowout Control
7 Drives and Stimulations
8 Directional Wells
9 Jobs on the Rig

(*The Petroleum Programme: English for the oil industry* by P. L. Sandler, BBC, 1980)

b) *Structural/situational syllabus*

1 The Hotel and Staff (1)
    Patterns of the verb 'to be'; demonstratives; personal pronouns.
2 The Hotel and Staff (2)
    Questions with 'where?'; some prepositions.

Application

3 Marcel in the Restaurant (1)
   Adjectives; 'either or', 'neither nor'.

4 Marcel in the Restaurant (2)
   Present Continuous Tense.

5 The Staff and the Customer
   Possessive adjectives and pronouns; questions with 'where?'

6 The Hotel at Night
   'There is,' 'there are', 'some', 'any', 'no', (1); questions with 'how many?'; the time (1)

7 The Manager
   'some', 'any', 'no' (2); the time (2)

8 The Kitchen (1)
   Patterns of the verb 'to have'

(The Savoy English Course for the Catering Industry by M. C. Coles and B. D. Lord, Edward Arnold, 1973)

c) *Functional/notional syllabus*

1 Properties and shapes
2 Location
3 Structure
4 Measurement 1
5 Process 1 Function and ability
6 Process 2 Actions in sequence
7 Measurement 2 Quantity
8 Process 3 Cause and Effect
9 Measurement 3 Proportion
10 Measurement 4 Frequency, Tendency, Probability
11 Process 4 Method

(Nucleus: General Science by M. Bates and T. Dudley-Evans, Longman, 1976)

d) *Skills syllabus*

1 Organising your studies
2 Improving your reading efficiency
3 Taking notes
4 Taking part in seminars
5 Writing an essay i) Research and using the library
6 Writing an essay ii) Organisation
7 Writing an essay iii) Presentation
8 Assessment, study techniques and examinations

(Study Skills in English by Michael J. Wallace, Cambridge University Press, 1980)

e) *Situational syllabus*

1 Schweibur: The Fiftieth Anniversary
2 The Sales Report
3 The Thanking Letter
4 A Telephone Message
5 A Death to Report
6 A Memo
7 A Journey
8 Minutes
9 An Article and a Memo
10 The Transfer
11 Changing Jobs
12 The New Secretary

(*English for Secretaries*, Oxford University Press, 1978)

f) *Functional/task-based syllabus*

1 Making arrangements
2 Attending meetings
3 Taking part in interviews
4 Buying and selling
5 Dealing with orders
6 Dealing with forms
7 Using the telephone
8 Dealing with international payments
9 Recording and decoding information
10 Travelling
11 Reporting
12 Receiving visitors

(*English for the Business and Commercial World: Career Developments* by
J. A. Blundell, N. M. G. Middlemiss, Oxford University Press, 1982)

g) *Discourse/skills syllabus*

UNIT 2
Generalizations

Part 1 The nature of generalizations
Part 2 General and specific information (paragraphs containing a single generalization)
Part 3 Levels of generality
Part 4 Levels of generality expressed by probability, frequency and quality
Part 5 Application of reading strategies to a passage with different levels of generality

(*Reading and Thinking in English: Discovering Discourse* ed. H. G. Widdowson,
Oxford University Press, 1979)

h) Skills and strategies

Unit one: Who do you think you are?
Exercises in personal evaluation

Unit two: What do you think you'll do?
Exercises in examining your job needs
Part 1 The hours you work
Part 2 Job security
Part 3 Making decisions
Part 4 Changing fields

Unit three: What will you find out?
Exercises in using the want ads
Part 1 An introduction to the want ads
Part 2 Want ad abbreviations
Part 3 The information in an ad
Part 4 Your qualifications
Part 5 Answering an ad

(*It's Up To You*: by J. Dresner, K. Beck, C. Morgano and L. Custer,
Longman Inc., 1980).*

Each of the syllabuses shown represents a valid attempt to break down
the mass of a particular area of knowledge into manageable units. Each
carries certain assumptions about the nature of language and learning.
But these assumptions may not be very explicit. For example, what
assumptions underlie the ordering in the structural syllabus (b)? Does
the verb 'to be' come first, because it is easier to learn? If so, in what
sense? Structurally, it is the most complex verb in English. Does it come
first because it is needed for later structures, for example the present
continuous? Is it considered to be conceptually simpler? For many
students, for example Indonesian students, it causes conceptual problems,
since in Bahasa Indonesian it is frequently omitted. Alternatively, is the
syllabus ordered according to usefulness? The verb 'to be' is more useful
than, say, the present simple tense of the verb 'to go'. If we are operating
the criterion of usefulness, what context are we referring to? Do we mean
usefulness in the outside world or usefulness in the classroom?

What about the functional/notional syllabus (c)? Does the order
imply that Describing Properties and Shapes is more common or more
fundamental than Describing Function and Ability? Or is there a covert
structural syllabus underlying the ordering? Describing Properties and

---

* Syllabus (h) illustrates an interesting feature of the American tradition of ESP. It has an avowed
social as well as a linguistic aim. 'Many students face the challenge of competing for jobs before
they feel proficient in English. *It's Up To You* is a novel approach to developing the language
skills and job-seeking strategies of these students.' (J. Dresner *et al.*, 1980) The aim is, therefore,
not just to improve language skills, but the much broader aim of enabling the learners to survive
and compete more effectively in American society. This reflects the strong influence in the USA
of concern for refugee and immigrant needs. This is why in America ESL tends to be used as
the umbrella term for English Language Teaching. In Britain, where the teaching of immigrants
is a relatively minor element in ELT, EFL is used as the umbrella term.

Shapes only requires the verb 'to be' (e.g. It is round/square/hard/soft etc.). Describing Function and Ability, on the other hand, requires can / can't / has the ability to…etc.

The syllabuses shown above are as important for what they don't say, as for what they do say, because they only show one or two of the elements of the materials. Any teaching materials must, in reality, operate several syllabuses at the same time. One of them will probably be used as the principal organising feature, but the others are still there, even if they are not taken into account in the organisation of the material. For example, every function is realised by one or more structures, thus in writing a functionally organised syllabus, a structural syllabus (good or otherwise) is automatically produced. Texts must be about something, thus all textbooks have willy-nilly a topic syllabus. Similarly, exercises demand the use of certain language processing skills: so, in writing a sequence of exercises, a skills syllabus of sorts is generated.

The syllabus that you see is only a statement of the criteria used to organise the mass of language use into a linear progression. Behind the stated syllabus are the other syllabuses, acknowledged by the authors or not, as the case may be.

We concluded chapters 3 and 4 by proposing a varied approach: taking from the various descriptions of language and theories of learning that which would most benefit the learning process. We showed an extract from a Business English syllabus that goes some way towards representing the variety of factors in the syllabus (figure 6). The developments of recent years in linguistics and psychology may not have given us any firm answers, but what they have done is show us that there is no single answer. There are different aspects and levels of language. There are different aspects and levels of learning. We don't know yet how they interrelate, but we do know that they exist. This knowledge should be reflected in a syllabus. If we know that there is both a functional and a structural aspect to language, then a course should have a functional and a structural syllabus. If we know that language knowledge is limited unless the learner has the skills and strategies for using it, then a course should have a skills and strategies syllabus too.

Any syllabus which claims to teach people how to communicate (in whatever specialised area) should acknowledge the complexity of communication. A syllabus that is framed in only one aspect (be it structures, functions, content or whatever) will probably miss the opportunity to develop the unacknowledged elements effectively. As Swan (1985b) says, when reviewing the structural/functional debate:

'The real issue is not which syllabus to put first: it is how to integrate eight or so syllabuses (functional, notional, situational, topic, phonological, lexical, structural, skills) into a sensible teaching programme.'

4 What role should a syllabus play in the course design process?

We can look at this question in terms of the approaches to course design that we outlined in chapter 6.

a) A language-centred approach

In this approach the syllabus is the prime generator of the teaching materials, as this model shows:

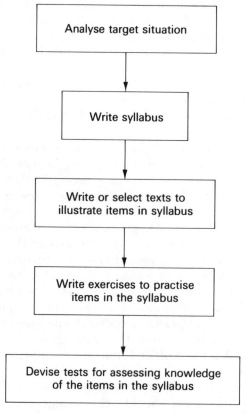

Figure 22: The role of the syllabus in a language-centred approach

This sort of approach is still widely used in ESP. The syllabus is quite clearly the determiner of the entire course. It is, so to speak, the crystallisation of what the course is all about – the inspiration for the production of texts and exercises and the basis on which proficiency will be evaluated.

b) A skills-centred approach

An alternative approach is needed in a skills-centred syllabus, since the aim is not to present and practise language items, but rather to provide opportunities for learners to employ and evaluate the skills and strategies considered necessary in the target situation. A skills-centred approach will often lay great store by the use of 'authentic' texts (see chapter 13, p. 158). A skills-centred approach to the use of the syllabus is suggested by Holmes (1981):

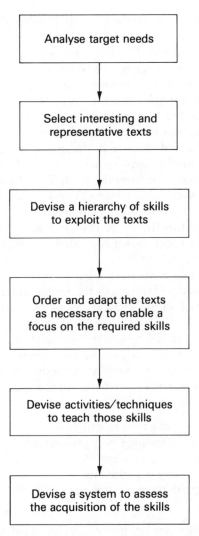

Figure 23: The role of the syllabus in a skills-centred approach

Application

In this approach the syllabus is not a prime generator. Although Holmes presents it as a linear process, it is more likely that there is a degree of negotiation between texts and skills. Thus, for example, the skills syllabus, as well as establishing criteria for the ordering and adaptation of texts, will probably also play a role in their initial selection. At the same time, the texts available will affect what can be focussed on in exercises and assessment.

c) A learning-centred approach

It will be noticeable that in the two approaches described so far the learning activities (tasks, exercises, teaching techniques) are almost the last factor to be considered. This may produce materials which faithfully reflect the syllabus in language or skills content, but it has a very constricting effect on the methodology. Learning, however, is more than just a matter of presenting language items or skills and strategies. In other words, it is not just the content of what is learnt that is important but also the activity through which it is learnt (Prabhu, 1983).

In a learning-centred approach the methodology cannot be just grafted on to the end of an existing selection of syllabus items and texts: it must be considered right from the start. To achieve this, the syllabus must be used in a more dynamic way in order to enable methodological considerations, such as interest, enjoyment, learner involvement, to influence the content of the entire course design. The simplest way of achieving this is to break down the syllabus design process into two levels (see figure 24).

The ESP syllabus is, as we have seen, usually derived from a detailed analysis of the language features of the target situation. It is the detail of this analysis which in our view produces the restricting influence on the methodology. But this need not occur. It is unnecessary to analyse language features in detail before the materials are started. A general syllabus outlining the topic areas and the communicative tasks of the target situation is all that is required at the beginning. For example, a general syllabus for technician students might look like this:

Topics	Tasks
names of tools	expressing use and purpose
electricity	understanding safety instructions
pumps	describing a system
materials	reporting experiments
construction	describing measurements
etc.	etc.

This general syllabus can be used as the basis for the initial selection of texts and writing of exercises/activities: it has enough detail to guide

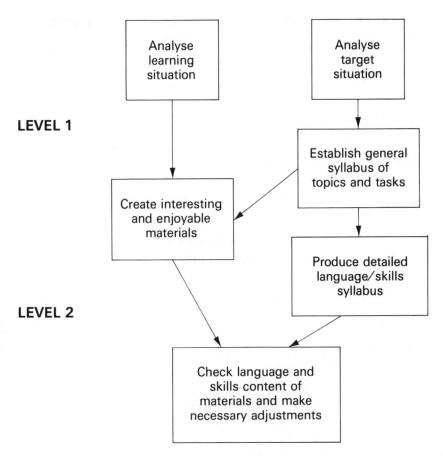

Figure 24: The role of the syllabus in a learning-centred approach

the materials writer, but not so much as to stifle creativity. It, therefore, allows the materials writer to take full account of factors emerging from the analysis of the learning situation.

The materials themselves will produce a detailed language syllabus. This materials-generated syllabus can then be checked against an independent syllabus produced from the needs analysis. Gaps and overlaps can then be dealt with.

Thus, instead of using the syllabus as the initial and once-for-all determiner of the content of materials and methodology, syllabus and materials evolve together with each being able to inform the other. In this way the syllabus is used creatively as a generator of good and relevant learning activities rather than as just a statement of language content which restricts and impoverishes the methodology. Yet, at the same time it maintains relevance to target needs. It, therefore, serves the needs of the students both as *users* and as *learners* of the language. The syllabus acts in the first instance as a compass to show the general direction. Then it becomes a sketch map. When the possibilities have been explored, obstacles noted and available resources collected, more detail can be filled in on the map, until the route is clear.

d) The post hoc approach

There is, of course, one last way of using the syllabus, which is probably more widespread than we might suppose:

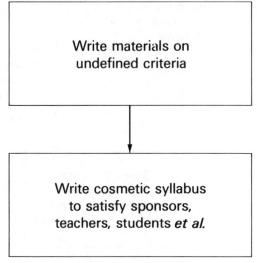

Figure 25: The role of the syllabus in a post hoc approach

Conclusion

In the institutionalised frameworks in which most teaching takes place, we must accept the predetermined syllabus as a fact of life. In view of the many roles that it plays it is essential that a great deal of thought is given to how the syllabus is used. It can, and unfortunately often does, act as a ball and chain, denying creativity and subjecting everything to evaluation criteria. But used sensibly and sensitively a syllabus can provide the support and guidance that creativity thrives on. A syllabus is not divine writ. It is a working document that should be used flexibly and appropriately to maximise the aims and processes of learning.

Tasks

1 What do *you* use a syllabus for?

2 Make a table of the advantages and disadvantages of having a syllabus.

3 'A syllabus is a statement of an ideal.' How far would you agree with this? What implications does it have for the use of the syllabus?

4 How can the ESP course designer take account of the 'learner syllabus'?

5 Choose one of the syllabuses given above. What assumptions about language and learning do you think underlie the ordering in it?

6 Study an ESP textbook that you know. On what criteria has it been organised? What 'hidden syllabuses' can you find?

9 Materials evaluation

> We must grant the artist his subject, his idea, his donné: our
> criticism is applied only to what he makes of it.
>
> (Henry James: *The Art of Fiction*)

Having completed your needs analysis and course design, you must now
decide what you are going to do with it. One option, of course, is to
decide that the whole thing is completely impossible and throw the
results in the wastepaper bin. Assuming, however, that you wish (or
have) to proceed, there are three possible ways of turning your course
design into actual teaching materials:
a) Select from existing materials: materials evaluation.
b) Write your own materials: materials development.
c) Modify existing materials: materials adaptation.
In this and the following chapter we shall look at the first two options:
materials evaluation and materials writing. The third option is a
combination of the first two. So, if this is your choice, you will need
to use both processes. Although we shall look at evaluation and
development separately, they are complementary activities. The materials
writer can learn a lot in terms of ideas and techniques from evaluating
existing materials. Similarly, writing materials makes you more aware
of what to look for in materials written by other people – and also more
sympathetic to the efforts of other materials writers!

1 Why evaluate materials?

Evaluation is a matter of judging the fitness of something for a particular
purpose. Given a certain need, and in the light of the resources available,
which out of a number of possibilities can represent the best solution?
Evaluation is, then, concerned with relative merit. There is no absolute
good or bad – only degrees of fitness for the required purpose.

In any kind of evaluation, the decision finally made is likely to be the
better for being based on a systematic check of all the important
variables. The results of an evaluation will probably lead to a large
investment of money in a published course or a large investment of time

in home-produced or adapted materials. Once such an investment is made, you will probably have to live with the consequences of it for some time, even if it later proves to have been a bad choice. A careful evaluation, then, can save a lot of expense and frustration. On the positive side, it can also help in justifying requests to sponsors or other members of an ESP team for money to buy materials or time to write them.

2 How do you evaluate materials?

Evaluation is basically a matching process: matching needs to available solutions. If this matching is to be done as objectively as possible, it is best to look at the needs and solutions separately. In the final analysis, any choice will be made on subjective grounds. If you were choosing a car, for example, you might just as easily choose it because you like the look of it as because it can reach 100 mph in 10 seconds. It depends on what you consider to be important. The danger is that, if subjective factors are allowed to influence judgement too soon, it may blind you to possibly useful alternatives. You might not look at cars from a particular country, because you have a prejudice against that country, while in fact those cars may suit your needs best. Similarly you might reject a particular textbook, because you don't like the picture on the cover, or because you dislike functional syllabuses. An ESP textbook has to suit the needs of a number of parties – teachers, students, sponsors, so it is important that the subjective factors, which will admittedly play a part, should not be allowed to obscure objectivity in the early stages of analysis.

   We can divide the evaluation process into four major steps (see figure 26):
1 Defining criteria.
2 Subjective analysis.
3 Objective analysis.
4 Matching.
Most of the work of the first two stages will have been done in the course design stage. It will be useful, however, to set out your criteria and your own preferred realisations of the criteria in a form which will make it easy to compare different sets of materials. Don't, however, see your own subjective analysis as a fixed set of requirements. You should use the materials evaluation process as a means of questioning and developing your own ideas as to what is required (Hutchinson, 1987, forthcoming). It is also very important to have some kind of rank order of factors. It is almost certain that there will be a conflict: one textbook might match your criteria in terms of content and language areas, but another might

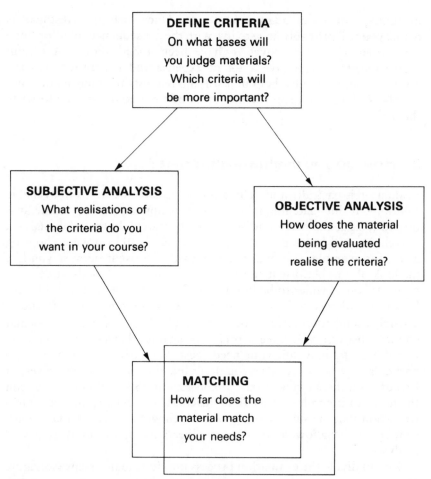

Figure 26: The materials evaluation process

have the more appropriate methodology. How will you make a choice? You will need to decide which you think is the more important to the various people concerned: teachers, students, sponsors. You should also consider which unsatisfactory features are easier to remedy. Is it, for example, easier to adapt content or methodology? You might find it difficult to find alternative texts, while it may be relatively easy to change the exercises based on the texts.

We can now present our own checklist of criteria for objective and subjective analyses. This is not an exhaustive list. You may find other criteria which you feel are important.

SUBJECTIVE ANALYSIS	OBJECTIVE ANALYSIS
(i.e. analysis of your course, in terms of materials requirements)	(i.e. analysis of materials being evaluated)

AUDIENCE

1A Who are your learners?
e.g.
– ages
– sex
– nationality/ies
– study or work specialism(s) (e.g. banking, medicine etc.)
– status/role with respect to specialism (e.g. trainee cashier, qualified anaesthetist etc.)
– knowledge of
  (i) English
  (ii) specialism
  (iii) other (e.g. knowledge of 'the world' etc.)
– educational backgrounds
– interests *(etc.)*
	1B Who is the material intended for?

AIMS

2A What are the aims of your course?	2B What are the aims of the materials? *(Note:* check that the aims are actually what they are said to be, by looking carefully at the material itself.)

⟫⟶

<table>
<tr><th>SUBJECTIVE
ANALYSIS</th><th>OBJECTIVE
ANALYSIS</th></tr>
</table>

CONTENT

3A What kind of *language description* do you require? Should it be structural, notional, functional, discourse-based, some other kind, a combination of one or more of these? (see ch.4).	3B What type(s) of linguistic description is/are used in the materials?
4A What *language points* should be covered? (i.e. What particular structures, functions, vocabulary areas etc?)	4B What language points do the materials cover?
5A What *proportion of work on each macro-skill* (e.g. reading) is desired? Should there be skills-integrated work?	5B What is the proportion of work on each skill? Is there skills-integrated work?
6A What *micro-skills* do you need? (e.g. deducing the meanings of unfamiliar words – see Munby (1978), pages 116–132)	6B What micro-skills are covered in the material?
7A What *text-types* should be included? e.g. – manuals? – letters? – dialogues? – experimental reports? – visual texts (pictures, diagrams, charts, graphs, cartoons etc.)? – listening texts? – any other kind?	7B What kinds of texts are there in the materials?

8A What *subject-matter* area(s) is/are required (e.g. medicine, biology etc.)?

What *level of knowledge* should be assumed (e.g. secondary school, first year college/university, post-graduate etc.)?

What types of *topics* are needed? (e.g. in medicine: hospital organisation, medical technology etc.)?

What *treatment* should the topics be given (e.g. 'straightforward', factual; 'human interest' angle; humorous; unusual perspective; taking into account issues, controversy, *etc.*)

8B What is/are the subject-matter area(s), assumed level of knowledge, and types of topics in the materials?

What treatment are the topics given?

9A How should the content be *organised throughout the course?*
  – around language points?
  – by subject-matter?
  – by some other means (e.g. study skills)?
  – by a combination of means?

9B How is the content organised throughout the materials?

10A How should the content be *organised within the course units?*

  – by a set pattern of components?
  – by a variety of patterns?
  – by some other means?
  – to allow a clear focus on e.g. certain skill areas, a communication task etc.?

10B How is the content organised within the units?

11A How should the content be *sequenced throughout the course?*
  e.g. – from easier to more difficult?
    – to create variety?
    – to provide recycling?
    – by other criteria?
  Should there be no obvious sequence?

11B How is the content sequenced throughout the book?

⫸➝

SUBJECTIVE ANALYSIS	OBJECTIVE ANALYSIS

12A How should the content be *sequenced within a unit?*
e.g. – from guided to free?
    – from comprehension to production?
    – accuracy to fluency? (see Brumfit, 1984, p.52–7)
    – by some other means?
Should there be no obvious sequence?
	12B How is the content sequenced within a unit?

METHODOLOGY

SUBJECTIVE ANALYSIS	OBJECTIVE ANALYSIS
13A What *theory/ies of learning* should the course be based on? Should it be behaviourist, cognitive, affective, some other kind, a combination of one or more of these? (See ch.5)	13B What theory/ies of learning are the materials based on? (Check carefully – don't just take the author's or publisher's word for it!)
14A What aspects of the *learners' attitudes to / expectations about learning English* should the course take into account? (See ch.6)	14B What attitudes to / expectations about learning English are the materials based on?
15A What *kinds of exercises/tasks* are needed? e.g. – guided ⟷ free? – comprehension ⟷ production? – language/skills practice ⟷ language/skills use? – one right answer ⟷ many possible right answers? – whole class ⟷ group ⟷ individual?	15B What kinds of exercises/tasks are included in the materials?

- language-/skills-based ⟷ content-based?
- 'mechanical' ⟷ problem-solving?
- role-play, simulation, drama, games?
- ones involving visuals?
- self-study?
- some other kinds?

16A What *teaching-learning techniques* are to be used?
e.g.
- 'lockstep'?
- pair-work?
- small-group work?
- student presentations?
- work involving technical subject-matter?
- other kinds?

16B What teaching-learning techniques can be used with the materials?

17A What *aids* are available for use?
e.g.
- cassette recorders?
- overhead projectors?
- realia?
- wallcharts?
- video?
- other?

17B What aids do the materials require?

18A What *guidance/support for teaching the course* will be needed?
e.g.
- statements of aims?
- lists of vocabulary and language-skills points?
- language guidance?
- technical information?
- methodological directive or hints?
- suggestions for further work?
- tests?
- other kinds?

18B What guidance do the materials provide?

⟫→

SUBJECTIVE ANALYSIS	OBJECTIVE ANALYSIS
19A How *flexible* do the materials need to be?	19B In what ways are the materials flexible? e.g. – can they be begun at different points? – can the units be used in different orders? – can they be linked to other materials? – can they be used without some of their components (e.g. cassettes)?

OTHER CRITERIA

SUBJECTIVE ANALYSIS	OBJECTIVE ANALYSIS
20A What price range is necessary?	20B What is the price?
21A When and in what quantities should the materials be available? *etc.*	21B When and how readily can the materials be obtained? *etc.*

Figure 27: A checklist for materials evaluation

The following steps should be followed in using the checklist:
1 Answer the A questions first to identify your requirements. You can then use this information either as a basis for writing your own materials or as input to the later stages of materials evaluation.
2 Analyse the materials you have selected by answering the B questions. If possible, test your ideas by teaching extracts from the materials.
3 Compare the A and B findings. This can be done impressionistically or by awarding points:
   o = does not match the desired feature
   1 = partly matches the desired feature
   2 = closely matches the desired feature

Total the points and analyse the results. Note that the highest number of points does not necessarily indicate the most suitable materials, since the points may be concentrated in one area. Look for the widest spread of desired features and concentrations in the areas you consider most important.

4 Make your choice and use your findings to prepare any documentation needed for defending your decision.

Conclusion

In this chapter we have looked at materials evaluation as one way of exploiting a course design. Even if you eventually decide to write your own materials, the evaluation of existing materials can provide a good source of ideas (of what to avoid as well as what to do) and techniques. It can also save a lot of duplication of effort by possibly revealing existing materials that can provide all or part of your materials needs. The evaluation process should be systematic and is best seen as a matching exercise: matching your analysed needs with available solutions.

But within all of us there is said to be an author struggling to get out. In the next chapter we shall present some techniques to help the aspiring materials writer.

Tasks

1 What can the ESP teacher learn from an evaluation of materials?

2 What criteria would you regard as the most important in evaluating materials? Put the categories in the checklist in a rank order of importance.

3 Try out the checklist for your own ESP situation. Fill in the objective analysis for your course. Then choose a textbook or set of materials and do the subjective analysis. Prepare a report on why you would choose or reject the material. (You never know, you might find the perfect textbook for your course!)

10 Materials design

A man may write at any time, if he will set himself doggedly
to it.

(Samuel Johnson)

Materials writing is one of the most characteristic features of ESP in
practice. In marked contrast to General English teaching, a large amount
of the ESP teacher's time may well be taken up in writing materials.
There are a number of reasons for this:
a) A teacher or institution may wish to provide teaching materials that
   will fit the specific subject area of particular learners. Such materials
   may not be available commercially. In addition to the profusion of
   subject specialisms, there is also a wide range of course types.
   Whereas schools, for example, work to standard timetables with a
   similar number of hours, ESP courses can vary from one week of
   intensive study to an hour a week for three years or more. Publishers
   are naturally reluctant to produce materials for very limited markets.
   The cost of producing and marketing a book is much the same
   regardless of whether it sells one thousand copies or one hundred
   thousand copies. It is likely, then, that a course tailored to the needs
   of a specific group of ESP learners will not be available.
b) Even when suitable materials are available, it may not be possible to
   buy them because of currency or import restrictions.
c) ESP materials may also be written for non-educational reasons: for
   example, in order to enhance the reputation of an institution or an
   individual. Materials are a visible product of activity, regardless of
   whether such activity is useful or even necessary.
For these and other reasons, there is already an established tradition of
ESP teachers producing in-house materials. These may then be distributed
to other institutions or even published, but in general they are written
by the teachers of a particular institution for the students at that
institution. Such a pattern of work is often something of an abuse of
teachers. Few have had any training in the skills and techniques of
materials writing. It also shows a rather cavalier attitude to the activity
of materials writing, implying, as it does, that if you can teach you can
write materials. How many actors are expected to write their own plays

or singers their own songs? On the other hand, it can be argued that the process of materials writing may help to make teachers more aware of what is involved in teaching and learning.

Rightly or wrongly, materials writing is a fact of life for a large number of ESP teachers, and so, accepting this fact, let us look at some techniques for producing useful and creative ESP materials.

1 Defining objectives

We can start by asking ourselves the question: What are materials supposed to do? In defining their purpose, we can identify some principles which will guide us in the actual writing of the materials.

a) Materials provide a stimulus to learning. Good materials do not teach: they encourage learners to learn. Good materials will, therefore, contain:
   - interesting texts;
   - enjoyable activities which engage the learners' thinking capacities;
   - opportunities for learners to use their existing knowledge and skills;
   - content which both learner and teacher can cope with.

b) Materials help to organise the teaching-learning process, by providing a path through the complex mass of the language to be learnt. Good materials should, therefore, provide a clear and coherent unit structure which will guide teacher and learner through various activities in such a way as to maximise the chances of learning. This structure should help the teacher in planning lessons and encourage in the learner a sense of progress and achievement. On the other hand, materials should not be so tightly structured as to produce a monotonous pattern of lessons – the curse of so many materials. Avoid the assembly line approach, which makes each unit look the same, with the same type of text, the same kind of illustrations, the same type and number of exercises. If it doesn't send you to sleep writing them, it will certainly send your learners to sleep using them. A materials model must be clear and systematic, but flexible enough to allow for creativity and variety.

c) Materials embody a view of the nature of language and learning. In writing materials you, as an author, are making all manner of statements about what you think language learning consists of. Materials should, therefore, truly reflect what you think and feel about the learning process. If you believe that people learn when their thinking capacities are engaged, don't write exercises which require little or no active thought. If you think learning is enhanced by intense experiences with language, don't provide texts which have been stripped of any human interest. If you think learning is helped by frequent reinforcement, make sure that items to be learnt are processed several times.

d) Materials reflect the nature of the learning task. We have noted in previous chapters that language learning is a complex process involving many different kinds and levels of knowledge. In the heyday of structuralism, it was assumed that a knowledge of the structures was the same as knowing a language and that repetition led to learning. Materials writing was a simple task of isolating the structure, writing a text to exemplify it and pattern drills to practise it. We must now take a more humble view and recognise that language learning is a very complex and little understood process. Materials should try to create a balanced outlook which both reflects the complexity of the task, yet makes it appear manageable.

e) Materials can have a very useful function in broadening the basis of teacher training, by introducing teachers to new techniques.

f) Materials provide models of correct and appropriate language use. We have deliberately placed this last on our list. This is a necessary function of materials, but it is all too often taken as the only purpose, with the result that materials become simply a statement of language *use* rather than a vehicle for language *learning*. Language teaching materials should not be the kind of beginner's guide to Applied Linguistics, which is so prevalent in ESP. We, as linguists, may be endlessly fascinated by the analysis of discourse: it is our chosen specialist field. For the doctor, the secretary and the engineer language may have little such attraction.

2   A materials design model

Taking into account the principles we have outlined, we can now present a model which we have used for writing our own materials. The aim of this particular model is to provide a coherent framework for the integration of the various aspects of learning, while at the same time allowing enough room for creativity and variety to flourish. The model consists of four elements: *input, content focus, language focus, task.*

a) *Input*: This may be a text, dialogue, video-recording, diagram or any piece of communication data, depending on the needs you have defined in your analysis. The *input* provides a number of things:
   – stimulus material for activities;
   – new language items;
   – correct models of language use;
   – a topic for communication;

- opportunities for learners to use their information processing skills;
- opportunities for learners to use their existing knowledge both of the language and the subject matter.

b) *Content focus*: Language is not an end in itself, but a means of conveying information and feelings about something. Non-linguistic content should be exploited to generate meaningful communication in the classroom.

c) *Language focus*: Our aim is to enable learners to *use* language, but it is unfair to give learners communicative tasks and activities for which they do not have enough of the necessary language knowledge. Good materials should involve both opportunities for analysis and synthesis. In *language focus* learners have the chance to take the language to pieces, study how it works and practise putting it back together again.

d) *Task*: The ultimate purpose of language learning is language use. Materials should be designed, therefore, to lead towards a communicative *task* in which learners use the content and language knowledge they have built up through the unit.

These four elements combine in the model as follows:

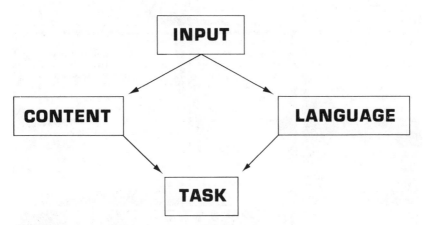

Figure 28: A materials design model

The primary focus of the unit is the *task*. The model acts as a vehicle which leads the learners to the point where they are able to carry out the *task*. The *language* and *content* are drawn from the *input* and are selected according to what the learners will need in order to do the *task*. It follows that an important feature of the model is to create coherence in terms of both language and content throughout the unit. This provides the support for more complex activities by building up a fund of knowledge and skills.

3   A materials design model: sample materials

The basic model can be used for materials of any length. Every stage could be covered in one lesson, if the *task* is a small one, or the whole unit might be spread over a series of lessons. In this part, we will show

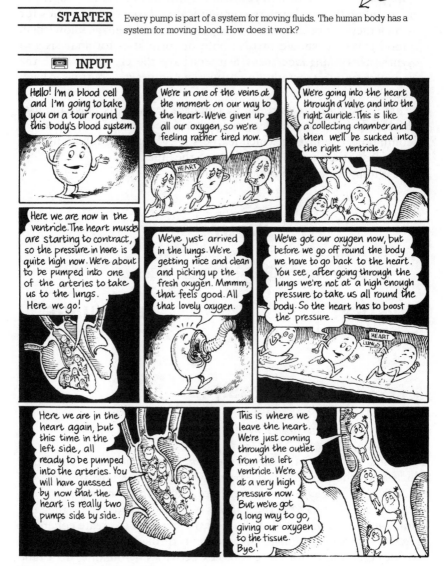

Figure 29a: Starter and input

what the model looks like in practice in some of our own materials. You will notice some additional features: these will be explained, as they arise.

The materials are intended for lower intermediate level students from a variety of technical specialisms. The topic of the blood circulation system can be of relevance to a wide range of subjects. Apart from the general human interest that any medical matter has, the lexis is of a very basic type that is generally applicable both literally and metaphorically (e.g. heart, artery, pump, collecting chamber, oxygen). Indeed there are only two specific terms used – ventricle and auricle. Thus the text is better viewed as an illustration of the general principles of fluid mechanics rather than as a medical text.

As the unit title indicates, language is approached through an area of content. The topic represents a common form of technical discourse – describing a circulatory system – although in this case, presented from an unusual point of view (see below p. 123).

The *starter* plays a number of important roles:
- It creates a context of knowledge for the comprehension of the *input*. Comprehension in the ESP classroom is often more difficult than in real life, because texts are taken in isolation. In the outside world a text would normally appear in a context, which provides reference points to assist understanding (Hutchinson and Waters, 1981).
- It activates the learners' minds and gets them thinking. They can then approach the text in an active frame of mind.
- It arouses the learners' interest in the topic.
- It reveals what learners already know in terms of language and content. The teacher can then adjust the lesson to take this into account.
- It provides a meaningful context in which to introduce new vocabulary or grammatical items.

GATHERING INFORMATION

STEP 1

Connect the two halves of the sentences to make true statements.

The heart	pumps blood to the lungs.
The veins	carry blood from the heart to the body tissue.
The auricles	is a kind of pump.
The right ventricle	carry blood to the heart.
The lungs	is pumped from the lungs back to the heart.
The fresh blood	pump blood into the ventricles.
The left side of the heart	supply the blood with oxygen.
The arteries	pumps the fresh blood into the arteries.

STEP 2

Copy this diagram of the heart and blood system.

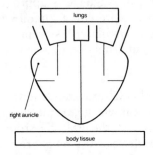

a   On your diagram label the auricles and ventricles.
b   Extend the blood vessels at the top of the heart to make a complete circulation diagram through the lungs and the body tissues.
c   Put in arrows to show the flow of blood through the system.

STEP 3

Use these expressions to replace those of similar meaning in the INPUT.

drawn; next to each other; increase; enter; get smaller; return; collect; exit; blood vessel (2).

📼 STEP 4   Listening task

a   One of the commonest forms of illness nowadays is heart disease. From what you have just learned about the heart, what do you think are the causes of heart failure?

b   Look at the pump in the TASK in Section A again. Just like the heart, there are several things that could go wrong with it. Make a table like this, and complete it with the information on the cassette.

Figure 29b: Gathering information

③ { This section practises extracting information from the *input* and begins the process of relating this content and language to a wider context.

④ { Steps 1 and 2 are not only comprehension checks. They also provide data for the later language work (steps 5 and 6). This is an example of unit coherence.

⑤ { Learners should always be encouraged to find answers for themselves wherever possible.

⑥ { It is possible to incorporate opportunities for the learners to use their own knowledge and abilities at any stage. It is particularly useful to do this as soon as the basic information contained in the *input* has been identified, in order to reinforce connections between this and the learners' own interests and needs. Here, for example, the learners are required to go beyond the information in the *input*. They have to relate the subject matter to their own knowledge and reasoning powers, but still using the language they have been learning.

》》》→

Application

LANGUAGE
FOCUS   STEP 5   Describing a system 1

Look at this description of how relief rainfall occurs.

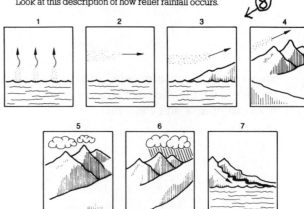

1   Water vapour from the sea rises.
2   The wind picks up the water vapour.
3   The wind carries the water vapour towards the mountains.
4   The mountains push the wet air upwards.
5   The temperature is lower up the mountains. The water vapour condenses into cloud.
6   The condensed water falls as rain.
7   The rain water runs down through rivers and streams to the sea.

This description is very simple. It follows the diagram in numbered stages, explaining what happens at each stage.

Make a similar description for the heart and blood system. On your diagram number the stages first, then write a sentence to explain each stage. Begin like this.

1   *Old blood goes into the right auricle.*
2   *The blood is sucked into the right ventricle.*
Continue.

STEP 6   Linking clauses

a   The description of relief rainfall is very simple, but there is a lot of repetition in it. We can make it much shorter like this.

Water vapour from the sea rises. The wind picks it up and carries it towards the mountains, which push the wet air upwards, where the temperature is lower. The water vapour condenses into clouds and falls as rain, which runs down through rivers and streams to the sea.

What changes have been made to shorten the description?

b   Make your description of the blood system shorter in the same way.

Figure 29c: Language focus

This section gives practice in some of the language elements needed for the *task*. These may be concerned with aspects of sentence structure, function or text construction. The points focussed on are drawn from the *input*, but they are selected according to their usefulness for the *task*.

 Further input related to the rest of the unit in terms of subject matter or language can be introduced at any point in order to provide a wider range of contexts for exercises and tasks. This helps learners to see how their limited resources can be used for tackling a wide range of problems (see also step 7).

⑨ Learners need practice in organising information, as well as learning the means for expressing those ideas.

⑩ Earlier work is recycled through another activity. This time the focus is more on the language form than the meaning.

⑪ Language work can also involve problem-solving with learners using their powers of observation and analysis (Hutchinson, 1984).

Application

STEP 7   Describing a system 2

This diagram shows the flow of water through a domestic central heating and hot water system.

Study the diagram and then describe the flow of water through the system.

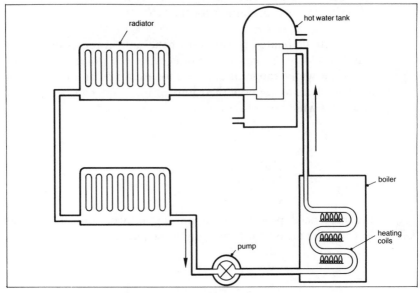

STEP 8   Tenses in descriptions

Note the difference between these two descriptions:

'We're going into the right auricle.'
The old blood goes into the right auricle.

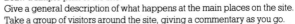

Why are different tenses used in the different situations?

Describe the relief rainfall cycle, as if you were a water molecule. Begin like this.

Hello, my name's H_2O, but you can call me H for short. I'm a water molecule and at the moment I'm floating around in the sunny Pacific, but it's very warm and I'm starting to evaporate ......
Continue.

TASK

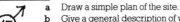

A tour around your place of study or work.

a   Draw a simple plan of the site.
b   Give a general description of what happens at the main places on the site.
c   Take a group of visitors around the site, giving a commentary as you go.

Figure 29d: Task

There is a gradual movement within the unit from guided to more open-ended work. This breaks down the learning tasks and gives the learners greater confidence for approaching the *task*.

⑬ The unusual type of *input* gives the opportunity for some more imaginative language work.

⑭ Here the learners have to create their own solution to a communication problem. In so doing they use both the language and the content knowledge developed through the unit. The learners, in effect, are being asked to solve a problem, *using* English, rather than to do exercises *about* English. Given the build-up through the unit, the *task* should be well within the grasp of both learner and teacher.

⑮ The *task*, also, provides a clear objective for the learners and so helps to break up the often bewildering mass of the syllabus, by establishing landmarks of achievement.

The unit can be further expanded to give learners the chance to apply the knowledge gained to their own situation. For example, a project for this unit could ask the learners to describe any other kind of enclosed system (e.g. an air conditioning system) in their own home, place of work or field of study.

4 Refining the model

A number of possible refinements to the model can be seen in the unit above. We can relate these points to the nucleus of the model to provide an extended model like this:

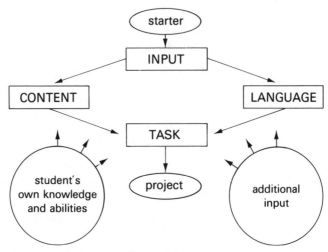

Figure 30: *An expanded materials model*

5 Materials and the syllabus

We noted in chapter 7 that, although one feature might be used as the organising principle of a syllabus, there are in fact several syllabuses operating in any course. We noted also when dealing with needs analysis in chapter 5 that we must take account not just of the visible features of the target situation, but also of intangible factors that relate to the learning situation, for example learner involvement, variety, use of existing knowledge etc. A model must be able to ensure adequate coverage through the syllabus of all the features identified as playing a role in the development of learning. In addition to having an internal coherence, therefore, each unit must also relate effectively to the other units in the course. There needs to be a coherence between the unit structure and the syllabus structure to ensure that the course provides adequate and appropriate coverage of syllabus items.

Figure 31 illustrates in a simplified form how the unit model relates to the various syllabuses underlying the course design. Note, however, that identifying features of the model with syllabus features does not mean that they only play a role in that position, nor that other factors are not involved in that position. The diagram aims to show the main focus of each element in the materials.

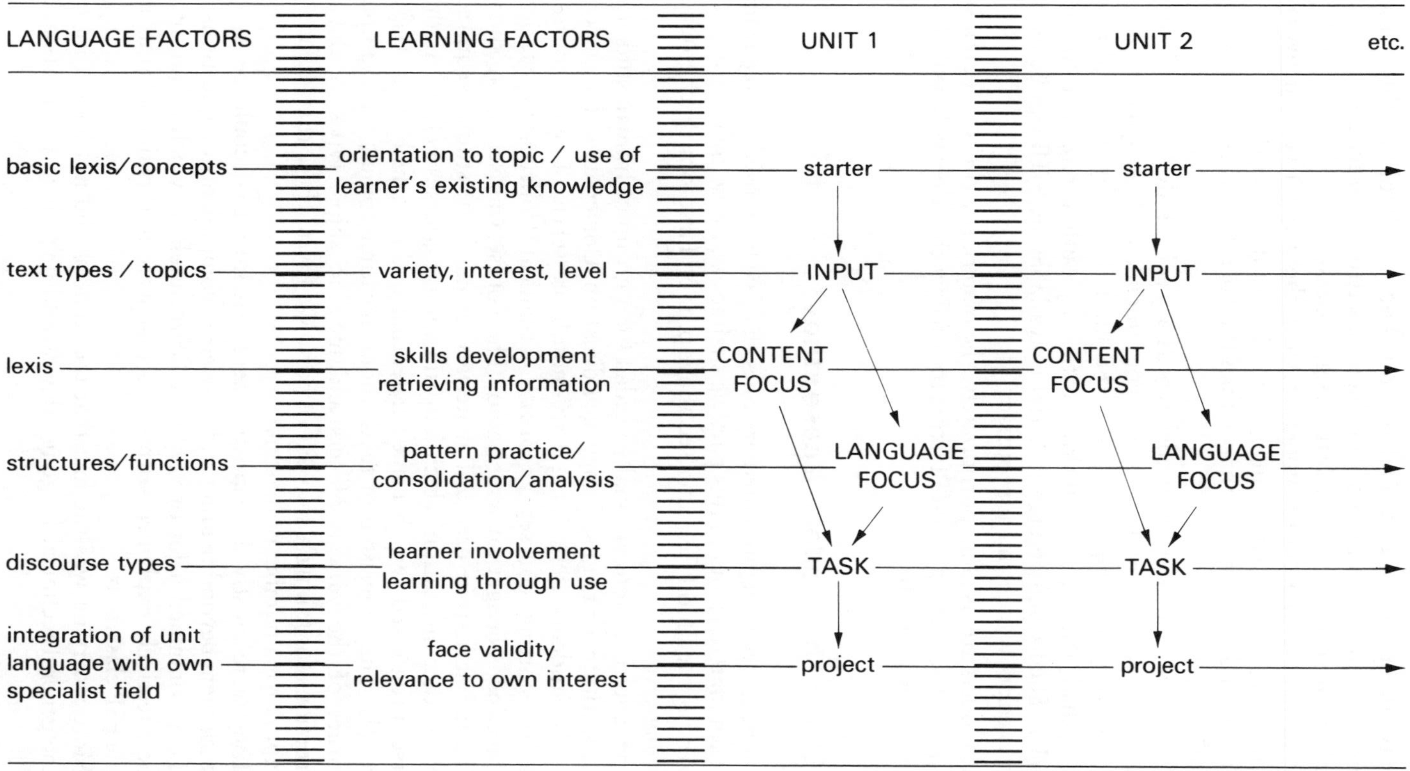

LANGUAGE FACTORS	LEARNING FACTORS	UNIT 1	UNIT 2	etc.
basic lexis/concepts	orientation to topic / use of learner's existing knowledge	starter	starter	
text types / topics	variety, interest, level	INPUT	INPUT	
lexis	skills development retrieving information	CONTENT FOCUS	CONTENT FOCUS	
structures/functions	pattern practice/consolidation/analysis	LANGUAGE FOCUS	LANGUAGE FOCUS	
discourse types	learner involvement learning through use	TASK	TASK	
integration of unit language with own specialist field	face validity relevance to own interest	project	project	

Figure 31: The syllabus/unit interface (S/UI)

We have made wide use of models throughout this book. At this point it is useful to make a cautionary distinction between two types of model, since both are used in the materials design process:

a) *Predictive*. This kind of model provides the generative framework within which creativity can operate. The unit model (Figure 26) is of this kind. It is a model that enables the operator to select, organise and present data.

b) *Evaluative*. This kind of model acts as a feedback device to tell you whether you have done what you intended. The syllabus/unit interface model (Figure 31) is of this kind. Typically it is used as a checklist. Materials are written with only outline reference to the S/UI. Then when enough material is available the S/UI can be used to check coverage and appropriacy.

If the models are used inappropriately, the materials writers will almost certainly be so swamped with factors to consider that they will probably achieve little of worth.

6 Using the models: a case study

The models we have presented are ones that we have used in preparing our own materials and in this part we shall look at how they were used in creating the Blood Cell unit (see above p. 110). First some background information:

The materials were originally needed for a group of Iranian students at the Institute for English Language Education, University of Lancaster, UK. The students were doing a six-month pre-service English course, prior to starting courses at British Technical Colleges in Marine Engineering, Navigation and Radio. The course was set up at short notice and at first we used ESP materials for maritime studies acquired from another institution which had run similar courses before. As the course progressed we became increasingly dissatisfied with these materials. They consisted of texts about maritime topics, for example the roles of the various officers and men on ships, types of ships, instructions for taking a ship out of port. We found these texts difficult to exploit for a number of reasons:

a) They were mostly descriptive. There was little that could be done with them beyond reading and answering comprehension questions.

b) They contained a lot of very specific vocabulary which could only be effectively explained with realia that were not available to us in the ESP classroom.

c) More worrying was the fact that the students did not have a lot of the general technical language that would help them to understand the specific language. For example, it is difficult to explain words like 'sheet', 'backspring' and 'rudder', if the students don't know words like 'rope' and 'steer'.

We decided to carry out a new needs analysis and go to the technical colleges, themselves. We discovered some interesting facts:

a) Although the students were going to study specific subjects such as marine engineering and navigation, 90% of the first year's work was on general technical topics (electricity, materials etc.), which were common to a very wide range of courses.

b) Lecturers assumed that on coming to the college students (whether native or non-native speakers) would know little or nothing about maritime matters, other than a few common words like 'cargo', 'sail', 'wave', 'tanker'.

c) In teaching the specific subjects, lecturers made wide use of references to non-maritime topics. For example, they would relate the parts of a ship to the parts of a car or a house. They might explain how a ship's air supply system works by reference to the blood system in the body. In other words, lecturers made use of an assumed level of competence in general areas in order to teach the new and specific knowledge (Hutchinson and Waters, 1980).

We concluded from our needs analysis that we had been teaching our students specific maritime language which they would not really need, while neglecting the general areas they would need. We were, in effect, giving them performance data, while neglecting the competence. Armed with this insight we set about creating the materials from which the Blood Cell unit was later developed.

Having established the background, we can now look in detail at the gestation process of the unit. We shall present this in the form of guidelines for using the models and illustrate them with our own procedure in producing the Blood Cell unit.

Stage 1: Find your text.

In selecting texts we operated three criteria:
- It should be a naturally occurring piece of communication or a piece that might well have occurred naturally. This would not exclude the possibility of adaptation or re-writing at a later stage, if we felt that would improve the pedagogic usefulness of the text.
- It should be suited to the learners' needs and interests.
- It should be capable of generating useful classroom activities.

The criteria did not require that texts should come from the target situation, although they could have done so.

One text that we found was the following:

Application

In the body's blood system the heart is the pump that does the vital job of circulating the blood to all parts of the body. The tubes or blood vessels which carry blood from the heart are known as arteries; the blood vessels that return the blood to the heart are the veins. The heart is really two pumps side by side. Each pump sucks blood from veins into a collecting chamber, the atrium or auricle, which then pushes the blood under high pressure into the ventricle below it. The ventricles pump the blood under high pressure into arteries. The pulse, which can be felt at various parts of the body, is caused by the simultaneous pumping action of the two ventricles.

Blood that has given up its oxygen to the tissues (deoxygenated blood) enters the heart through the right atrium. The right ventricle then pumps it to the lungs. Here it collects oxygen and returns through the veins to the left side of the heart to be pumped to the rest of the body before returning to the right atrium again. The double circulation is needed because the pressure at which the oxygenated blood leaves the lungs is too low. The pressure has to be boosted by re-pumping through the heart, so that it can pass round the body fast enough to supply the body tissues with the necessary oxygen.

A very important role is played by small flaps of skin at the exits of the heart and between the auricles and ventricles: these are one-way valves that prevent the blood going the wrong way. If these valves are faulty it has a serious effect on the health of the person.

(from *Penguin Book of the Natural World*)

Stage 2: Go to the end of the model. Think of a *task* that the learners could do at the end of the unit.

We decided on getting the learners to describe a similar enclosed pumping system, such as a central heating system, air conditioning system or the operation of a refrigerator. There was no need to define it any more closely at this stage. Our concern here was to assess the creative potential of the text for classroom activities.

Stage 3: Go back to the syllabus. Is the *task* the kind of activity that will benefit your learners?

In this case, the *task* matched, since we had identified 'describing a system' as a necessary discourse function that our students would have to carry out. One problem, however, was that we already had quite a lot of *tasks* of this type. But we could worry about that later.

Stage 4: Decide what language structures, vocabulary, functions, content the *input* contains. Which of these would be useful for the *task*, i.e. what aspects of language and content can be usefully focussed on in the exercises?

We identified:
- names of specific parts;
- present active;

– discourse linkers (relative clauses, after, then etc.);
– describing systems;
– relationship between text and diagram.
This did not seem like very much. The text was not proving to have a lot of creative potential.

Stage 5: Think of some exercises and activities to practise the items you have identified.

We decided on:
– a transfer activity (step 2), in which learners would extract the essential information from the text and use it in order to complete and label a diagram of the system.
– a reconstruction activity, in which learners use the diagram to reconstruct the original text. We were not very happy with this. It seemed a bit like regurgitation. The text was already fairly concise and so would require little summarising.
– exercises where learners write descriptions of other systems, for example relief rainfall, central heating, if this was not used for the *task*.
By this time we were having serious doubts about the usefulness of our original text for a number of reasons:
– It was not strikingly interesting in the first instance.
– It didn't seem to lend itself to a lot of classroom activities.
– There were few language items to focus on.
– We already had some examples of the potential *task*. So this aspect of the discourse syllabus was adequately covered in other units.
But everything should be given a second chance.

Stage 6: Go back to the *input*. Can it be revised in any way to make it more useful? Try out any revisions on your learners, if possible. If nothing emerges, put it in cold storage (never throw a text or an exercise away; you might find a use for it later!) and look for another text.

In our case, the flash of insight came: we re-wrote the text from the point of view of an individual blood cell and set it in the form of a cartoon strip.

Stage 7: Go through stages 1–6 again with the revised *input*.

It might seem at first sight that the only advantage of changing to the Blood Cell was to inject an element of humour (though this in itself is a positive factor). In fact the revision greatly increased the creative potential of the unit, by setting up a new dimension – the contrast between a general, formal description and an informal description happening at a specific point in time. This meant that the following were now possible:

a) We could have a new *task*, which focussed on the contrast between a general and an immediate description. Checking back to the syllabus showed that we had no other *tasks* like this yet. (Note the use here of the syllabus as a checking device.)

b) We did not have to throw away the original *task* ideas. We could use them in the exercises to practise language and/or content items. We could also still use the transfer activity (step 2).

c) We could have a number of exercises which would exploit the learners' ability to transfer information from the informal register of the *input* to that of a general academic description (steps 1, 5 and 6). This would help in developing an awareness of register.

d) We now had a good, realistic setting in which to practise the distinction between the present simple and continuous tenses, which we had not yet covered in our language syllabus. (Note again the use of the syllabus as a checking device.)

e) There was an opportunity for some light relief with a bit of creative writing from the point of view of a water molecule (step 8). It might be objected that some learners would be insulted by such work. This is certainly a point to bear in mind, although in our experience this kind of activity is welcomed by learners as a chance for some fun, especially if it occurs well into the course when more conventional activities are losing their appeal. There is, in any case, no compulsion to do the exercise. We would repeat a point made earlier: materials should be a stimulus. They should provide opportunities for classroom activities. There is a lot to be said for putting in more than can actually be covered. Some can be left out to suit the needs of different situations.

f) Of greatest importance was the work that could now be done to follow up step 2. Whereas previously the learners had simply recreated the *input*, now they had a much more creative activity. They were transferring the *input* content into the diagram in step 2, as before. Then the information in the diagram could be used as input to an exercise on discourse linkers (step 6). This gave added coherence to the unit by recycling work from one exercise into another. But the real benefit was that in doing this new series of exercises the learners were in effect creating *for themselves* the original descriptive text we had started with (see figure 32). This, we felt, was a much more creative and meaningful learning activity than simply reconstructing a given text.

Having revised our unit using the new text, we could proceed to the remaining stages of using the model and complete a workable version of the materials.

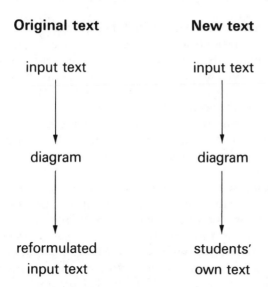

Original text

input text

↓

diagram

↓

reformulated
input text

New text

input text

↓

diagram

↓

students'
own text

Figure 32: A more creative learning task

Stage 8: Check the new materials against the syllabus and amend accordingly.

Stage 9: Try the materials in the classroom.

Stage 10: Most importantly, revise the materials in the light of classroom use. There is no such thing as perfect materials. They can always be improved.

Conclusion: Other options

In this chapter we have looked in detail at one of the most characteristic features of ESP work: materials writing. We have presented and shown how to operate a model which puts into practice a learning-centred approach to materials.

However, in concluding, we should state that for a number of reasons materials writing is best regarded as the last resort, when all other possibilities of providing materials have been exhausted.

a) We have noted that there is much common ground between learners of apparently very different subject specialisms. Thus you should first question whether the learners' needs are significantly different from those of other groups in your institution. It may be possible to use existing materials. But make sure that this solution is acceptable to everyone concerned. Students and sponsors might feel that they

are only getting their money's worth if they get a tailor-made course. Even so, a few strategic cosmetic changes may solve this problem.
b) If a new set of materials is needed, the second alternative is to look at published materials. You may not find one course which completely fits the bill, but a judicious selection of units from two or more courses may cover the needs of many students.
c) Even if the first two alternatives fail to provide exactly what you want, you can still try adapting existing material. You might add some exercises or change some of the texts to make them more appropriate to the learners' needs.
d) The final possibility is to try and reduce the area of the course that will require new materials. It is highly unlikely that any group of learners will require completely new materials for every lesson. Look at your course design and identify those areas that could be covered by existing materials (with or without adaptation). Then concentrate your materials writing effort on the remaining areas. You may well be surprised how little of the course will really need new materials.

For those who, in the end, feel they have to write new materials, here are a few hints:
a) Don't re-invent the wheel. Use existing materials as a source for ideas.
b) It's better to work in a team, if only to retain your sanity.
c) Don't set out to write the perfect materials on the first draft. Materials can always be improved. Do what you can and try it out. Use what you learn from this experience to revise and expand the materials.
d) Don't underestimate the time needed for materials writing. It can be a very time-consuming business.
e) Pay careful attention to the appearance of your materials. If they look boring and scruffy, they will be treated as such.
f) Good luck!

Tasks

1 The main purpose of ESP materials is to present models of correct language use in the target situation. How far would you agree with this?

2 What materials writing do you do? Why do you write your own materials?

3 Study your own ESP materials. What model underlies them?

4 Would the Blood Cell unit be suitable for your own ESP learners? Give reasons why or why not.

5 Look at the *task* at the end of the Blood Cell unit. What language and content knowledge is needed for it? How far is this knowledge covered through the unit?

6 Apply the syllabus/unit interface to the materials you use. Identify the syllabuses underlying your materials and try to match them to the various stages of your materials.

11 Methodology

I hear and I forget.
I see and I remember.
I do and I understand.

(Chinese proverb)

In chapter 4 we looked at various theories of learning and presented a model of learning. In this chapter we shall present three model lessons to illustrate the practical implications of these ideas for the classroom. First, however, let us extend the theoretical models we have considered and outline some basic principles of language learning, which will underpin a learning-centred methodology.

1 **Second language learning is a developmental process.** Learners use their existing knowledge to make the new information comprehensible. Only in this way can learning take place. 'Comprehension precedes learning' (Strevens, 1985). The learner's existing state of knowledge is, therefore, a vital element in the success or failure of learning, and the good teacher will consequently try to establish and exploit what the learners already know.

2 **Language learning is an active process.** It is not enough for learners just to *have* the necessary knowledge to make things meaningful, they must also *use* that knowledge. However, it is important to be clear what we mean by the term 'active'. We must make a distinction between two types of activity:

   a) *psycho-motor* activity, that is, the observable movement of speech organs or limbs in accordance with signals from the brain;

   b) *language processing* activity, that is, the organisation of information into a meaningful network of knowledge. This kind of activity is internal and not observable.

It is the language processing activity which is the important factor. If language is not connected into the network, the psycho-motor activity will have little if any benefit. In practical terms this means that 'activity' should not be judged in terms of how much learners say or write, but in terms of how much the learners have to think – to use their cognitive capacities and knowledge of the world to make sense of the flow of new information.

3 **Language learning is a decision-making process.** In the traditional classroom the teacher made all the decisions. Indeed it was essential for the teacher to do so in order to avoid all possibilities of error – you can't make decisions without taking risks and taking risks makes errors possible or even likely. But the process of developing and using a network of knowledge relies upon a train of learner decisions: What knowledge is new? How does it relate to the existing knowledge? What is the underlying pattern? Is there a rule of appropriacy here? Which bits of information are relevant? Which are unimportant? Learners must be decision-makers (see e.g. Allwright, 1978 a).

4 **Language learning is not just a matter of linguistic knowledge.** The most fundamental problem of second language learning is the mismatch between the learners' conceptual/cognitive capacities and the learners' linguistic level. In mother tongue learning they develop together. In the second language they are grossly out of focus: the second language learner is someone who is conceptually and cognitively mature, but is linguistically an infant. This is a particular problem in ESP, where the learners' knowledge of their subject specialism may be of a very high level, while their linguistic knowledge is virtually nil. Teaching must respect both levels of the learners' state (see e.g. Breen and Candlin, 1980).

5 **Language learning is not the learners' first experience with language.** Every second language learner is already communicatively competent in one language. They do not know the specific forms, words or possibly some of the concepts of the target language, but they know what communication is and how it is used (Swan, 1985 a). They may not be able to verbalise this knowledge, but it is there, for without it they would not be able to operate in their own mother tongue. Learners' knowledge of communication should be actively exploited in second language learning, for example, by getting students to predict, before reading or listening (see e.g. Widdowson, 1978).

6 **Learning is an emotional experience.** Our concern should be to develop the positive emotions as opposed to the negative ones by, for example:
   – using pair and group work to build on existing social relationships;
   – giving students time to think and generally avoiding undue pressure;
   – putting less emphasis on the *product* (the right answer) and more on the *process* of getting an answer;
   – valuing attitude as much as aptitude and ability;
   – making 'interest', 'fun', 'variety' primary considerations in materials and methodology, rather than just added extras.

7 **Language learning is to a large extent incidental.** You don't have to be working with language problems in order to learn language. You can learn a language incidentally, while you are actually thinking about

something else. The problems to be solved in a problem-solving approach do not have to be language problems (Prabhu, 1983). The important point is that the problems should oblige the learners to *use* language and thereby to fix the language into the matrix of knowledge in their minds (see e.g. Krashen, 1981).

8 **Language learning is not systematic.** We learn by systematising knowledge, but the process itself is not systematic. Laying out information in a systematic way will not guarantee learning. The learner must create an internal system. An external system may help, but that is all it can do.

In the model lessons that follow we shall show how these principles can be realised in the ESP classroom.

Model lesson 1

Materials

Worksheet 1 : Strip cartoon with bubbles blanked out.
Worksheet 2 : Bubble texts.
Tape of conversation.
A paperclip and a needle.

Audience

Engineering or General Technical students, intermediate level.

WORKSHEET 1

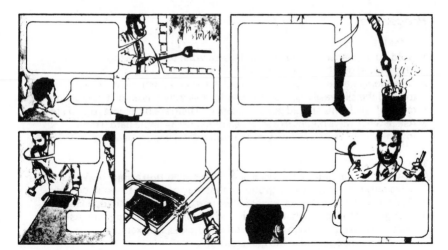

WORKSHEET 2

Figure 33: Model lesson 1: Worksheets 1 and 2

Application

Procedure

A STARTER:

1 Hold up the paperclip and the needle. Ask what they are made of. This should get the answer: 'steel'.
2 Give them to a student and ask him or her to bend them. He or she will be able to bend the clip easily, but not the needle. Ask why this is so, if they are both made of steel. This should get the answer: 'There are different types of steel.'
3 Ask in what ways metals like steel can differ, for example hard/soft, tough/brittle. You could ask what the different types are used for.

B ANALYSIS:

4 Divide the class into groups of 3 or 4. Give each group a copy of Worksheet 1. Give only one copy to each group, so that they will have to work together.
5 Tell the students to look at each picture and decide what is happening.
6 Ask groups to report what they think is happening in each picture. Ask questions to get as much information as possible, for example:

T: What is happening in the first picture?
S: A man is holding a piece of steel.
T: How do you know it is a piece of steel?
S: He says: 'This is a piece of mild steel.'
T: What about the second picture?
S: The man is holding a piece of steel again.
T: Is it the same piece of steel?
S: No, it looks different.
T: That could be a mistake in the drawing. Are there any other clues?
S: Yes, in the later pictures he mentions 'high carbon steel' and 'low carbon steel'.
T: Yes. OK.
etc.

C PREDICTION:

7 In this way students should build up enough facts to be able to predict what the dialogue is about. Ask the students who the people are; what the man is trying to do etc. In this way it should emerge that it is a teacher conducting an experiment to show the effects of heating and cooling on two types of steel.
8 Ask students to use the knowledge they now have and their knowledge of experiments to say what the stages in the experiment discourse will be, for example, 'The man is showing the materials, then he will probably explain what he is going to do, comment on his actions and draw a conclusion.'
9 Get the students to predict what the dialogue will be. What do they think will go in each bubble.
10 Groups suggest possible texts for the bubbles.

D MATCHING:

11 Give out Worksheet 2 (the bubble texts). Students put them in order to match the blank bubbles. If possible cut up Worksheet 2; students arrange bubbles in order.
12 Play the tape. Students check their versions.

E FOLLOW UP:

13 There are many possible ways of following this activity up:
   – Discuss the discourse pattern of experiments or the language.

– Students explain how they got their answers. What clues they used.
– Discuss the uses of different types of metals.
– Students write a report on the experiment.
– Give students pictures of another experiment. Get them to make a commentary or a report on it.
– Students do their own experiments.

Model lesson 2*

Materials

Worksheets 1, 2 and 3.
Feedback Worksheet.
(overhead projector foil of Feedback Worksheet)

Audience

Business or Secretarial students, upper intermediate/advanced level.

Procedure

A GATHERING INFORMATION:
1 Divide the class into groups of three and give each group a number: 1, 2, 3, 4 etc.
2 Give *one* of the worksheets to each group e.g.:

Group	Worksheet
1	1
2	2
3	3
4	1
5	2

etc.
3 Tell the groups to read their worksheets and make notes about the details, in particular writing down any information which answers the questions:
– Are any people mentioned? Who do you think they are?
– What is the communication about?
– Are any places mentioned? Why?
– Are any dates mentioned? What happened or will happen then?
– Are any items mentioned? How many?
For example, the notes for Worksheet 1 might look like this:
Mr Salgado and his secretary(?), Maria.
Mr Salgado wants Maria to call Lanka Shipping Services about typewriters from Birmingham, England. Wants to know arrival in Colombo.
Tell each member of the group to keep a copy of the notes, as they will be working in new groups in the second stage of the lesson.

* The materials for this lesson were developed by Tom Hutchinson as part of an ESP Project for Polytechnical Colleges in Sri Lanka.
    A video-recording of Tom Hutchinson teaching this lesson is available at the Institute for English Language Education, University of Lancaster.

Application

WORKSHEET 1

Mr Salgado:	Maria?
Maria:	Yes, Mr Salgado?
Mr Salgado:	Could you phone the shipping agents and find out when an order for some typewriters is due to arrive. They should be here soon.
Maria:	Yes, sir. What number is the order?
Mr Salgado:	It's order number B/123/45/E. It's for some typewriters from Olivetti in Birmingham, England.
Maria:	Ah yes, I remember it. It's being handled by Lanka Shipping Services, isn't it?
Mr Salgado:	Yes, that's right.
Maria:	And you want to know when the consignment will arrive in Colombo?
Mr Salgado:	Well, I really want to know when the consignment will be here at our warehouse. They'll have to unload the ship and clear the things through customs, before we can collect them.
Maria:	Very well, Mr Salgado. I'll chase it up.

WORKSHEET 2

LSS Clerk:	Good afternoon, LSS Ltd.
Miss Jayweera:	Good afternoon. This is Miss Jayweera from Metropolitan Agencies here. I'd like to know when an order you are handling for us will arrive. It's our reference B/123/45/E and it was placed on 30th March.
LSS Clerk:	Just a minute. Ah yes. The consignment left Liverpool two weeks ago.
Miss Jayweera:	So when will it arrive in Colombo?
LSS Clerk:	Let me see. It's Monday 18th July today, and it left on the 4th. So it should be here at the end of this week.
Miss Jayweera:	Friday?
LSS Clerk:	Say Saturday, to be safe.
Miss Jayweera:	And when can we collect the order?
LSS Clerk:	Give us a ring on Tuesday morning. It should be ready by then.
Miss Jayweera:	Thank you. Goodbye.
LSS Clerk:	Goodbye.

WORKSHEET 3   Polytechnical Institute,
                               Waidya Road,
                               Dehiwala.

                               12th March 1984

Metropolitan Agencies Ltd,
12 Sea View Road,
Colombo 7

Dear Sir,
   We should like to place an order with you for
the following item from your catalogue:

42 × Olivetti Omega typewriters (cat. no. TW/
952/Oli)

The price quoted in your catalogue is Rs 2800
per item. In view of the size of the order, we
feel that a reasonable discount could be offered
on this price. Please contact me so that we can
discuss the matter before you place the order
with your suppliers.

The typewriters will be needed for courses
beginning in September and it is therefore
imperative that they should arrive in good time
for this.

Thank you for your attention.

Yours Faithfully,

A. Gautamadasa
Principal

Figure 34: *Model lesson* 2: *Worksheets* 1, 2 *and* 3

Application

4   Go round the class and make sure that the students are noting down the relevant information and that they understand the facts of the text.
5   Collect the worksheets.

B   SHARING INFORMATION:
6   Form new groups of three, so that each new group has one member from each of the old groups. The simplest way to do this is to give each student in a group a letter. Then form new groups, by putting all the As together, all the Bs etc. Attach any odd students to other groups.

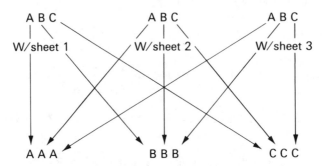

Figure 35: Cross-grouping

7   Check that each group has at least one member from each of the old groups. To do this, ask 'Who had Worksheet 1?' At least one hand in each group should be raised. This may seem tedious, but it will only take a few seconds and can save a lot of confusion.
8   Give one copy of the Feedback Worksheet to each group. Each member of the group has some of the missing information. Tell them to fill in the gaps using their notes.

C   FEEDBACK:
9   If you have an overhead projector, put the Feedback Worksheet onto a foil. Ask one group to complete it. Other groups compare their versions. Note that there may be more than one possible answer for some of the facts.
10 Discuss any differences in versions. Ask students how they worked out their answers.

D   FOLLOW UP:
11 Divide the class into pairs and get them to role play the conversation.
12 Get the students to compose a letter to Mr Gautamadasa, informing him about the delivery.

FEEDBACK WORKSHEET

Use the information you noted from Worksheets 1,
2 and 3 to complete this conversation.

Scene: Metropolitan Agencies Ltd.

..........: ...., did you find out when
those .... will arrive?

..........: Yes, ..., I phoned ....
.... this morning and
they said the ship should be here
....

..........: Where are they being shipped from?

..........: .... And the ship left
there on ....

..........: Hmmm. So the ship will be in Colombo
on .... or ....
They'll need a few days to unload the
cargo and clear customs, won't they?
So when will they be ready to collect?

..........: They should be ready ....

..........: Right. We'll have to test them, before
we can deliver them. How many
.... were ordered?

..........: ...., sir.

..........: It will take two days to test that
number. Can you telephone Mr
.... at ....
and tell him that we will deliver his
.... on Friday. What date
will that be?

..........: Friday next week will be ....

..........: Fine. Thank you, ...

Figure 36: *Model lesson* 2: *Feedback Worksheet*

Model lesson 3

Materials

Worksheet 1, cut into strips.
Worksheet 2.
Cassette recording of dialogue in Worksheet 1.

Audience

Hotel and tourist students, lower intermediate.

WORKSHEET 1

Good morning, Orient Hotel. Can I help you?
Good morning. I'd like to reserve a room for next week.
Yes, sir. Which days next week?
Monday to Friday, please.
And do you want a single or a double room?
A single with private bath.
All our rooms have private bathrooms, sir. Do you want full board?
No, just bed and breakfast, please.
So, that's a single room, bed and breakfast for four nights. Can I have your name and address, please?
It's Mr G. N. Jenkins, 14 Prince Street, Colombo.
Thank you, Mr Jenkins. Can you confirm the booking in writing before Monday?
Yes, I'll confirm it. Can you tell me how much the room will be?
Four hundred and fifty rupees a night, bed and breakfast, sir.
Thank you. Goodbye.
Goodbye, sir.

Figure 37: Model lesson 3: Worksheet 1

Procedure

A PREDICTION:
1 Play just the first line of the dialogue. '(*ring ring*) Good morning, Orient Hotel. Can I help you?'
2 Ask students to predict what the conversation is going to be about. Ask who is talking, what they think the caller wants, what the people in the dialogue might talk about. You will be surprised how much can be predicted from just one line. Introduce any new or important vocabulary.
3 Play the tape right through. Students listen and check their predictions.
4 Ask if there are any vocabulary difficulties.
5 Play the tape once more.

B RECONSTRUCTION:

6 Divide the class into pairs.
7 Give each pair the cut up dialogue. Their task is to put the dialogue back together again.
8 Go round and help students. Don't do it for them. Suggest ways in which they might find the answer, for example, by looking for repeated words.
9 Play the tape again. Students check their answers.
10 Play the tape one line at a time. Students repeat in chorus.

C PRACTICE:

11 Tell the students to write on each slip of paper who is speaking: receptionist or caller.
12 Tell one member of each pair to take the caller's pieces and the other to take the receptionist's pieces.
13 Pairs read the dialogue.
14 Tell the 'callers' to turn over their pieces of paper, so that they cannot see them. They do the dialogue again. Then the 'receptionists' turn their pieces over: the 'callers' turn theirs back. They do the dialogue again.
15 Collect the receptionist's pieces. Students must write the receptionist's part of the dialogue using the caller's part as cues.
16 Students role play their new conversations.
17 Give out Worksheet 2. Students make the dialogue for the new callers.

WORKSHEET 2

Mrs H. Peres phones the Hotel Paris.
She wants to reserve a double room for herself
and her husband for three nights from next
Wednesday. They will want full board and a
private bathroom.
Mr and Mrs Peres live at 35 Alfred Street,
Colombo.

Figure 38: Model lesson 3: Worksheet 2

Analysis

How do these lessons put into practice the principles outlined at the start of this chapter? They exploit a number of simple techniques, which can be applied to almost any lesson.

1 **Gaps.** If everything is certain and known, there is no need to think. Learning demands thinking. Gaps create that demand. There are many types of gap, which can be exploited:

   a) *Information gaps.* Most teachers will be familiar with this type of activity. One learner has some information, another does not. There is a need to communicate and share the knowledge.

b) *Media gaps.* The information is available in one medium and needs to be transferred to another medium, for example read: make notes: discuss using notes: complete gapped text.

c) *Reasoning gaps.* There are clues and pieces of evidence, but the answer needs to be extrapolated. Working out what the discourse is all about in lesson 1 is a good example of this.

d) *Memory gaps.* The learners have received some information at one stage of the lesson. Now they must use their memories to reconstruct. Reconstructing half the dialogue in lesson 3 exploits this kind of gap.

e) *Jigsaw gaps.* All the parts are there, but they need to be put together to form a complete unit.

f) *Opinion gaps.* What is important? What is not? What is relevant?

g) *Certainty gaps.* What is definitely known? What can be presupposed? What can be predicted? What is completely unavailable?

It is the gaps, the holes, the missing bits that seize the mind and trigger the thinking processes. A teacher's best friend can be the pair of scissors that creates the gaps which stimulate the learners' thinking processes.

2 **Variety.** It is the spice of learning. In order to get the repetition necessary to help learning, there must be variety to keep the mind alert. Variety can be achieved in a number of ways:

a) Variety of medium: text, tape, pictures, speech.

b) Variety of classroom organisation: whole class, pair, individual, group.

c) Variety of learner roles: presenter, evaluator, receiver, thinker, negotiator.

d) Variety of exercise, activity or task.

e) Variety of skills: reading, listening, writing, speaking, graphic skills.

f) Variety of topic.

g) Variety of focus: accuracy, fluency; discourse, structure, pronunciation etc.

3 **Prediction.** Prediction is a matter of using an existing knowledge of a pattern or system in order to anticipate what is likely in a novel situation. It is, therefore, central both to language use and language learning. Getting students to predict what will be in a piece of discourse has a number of practical pedagogic advantages, too:

a) It builds learner confidence by making them aware of their potential knowledge – of how much they really know about language, communication or the topic.

b) It enables the teacher to discover where the gaps in knowledge are, so that teaching can be made more relevant to needs.

c) It activates the learner's mind and prepares it for learning.

d) It gives students an ego investment. When people make predictions, they are investing part of their self-esteem in their decisions and choices. They are putting their ego on the line and taking risks. Having done so, the one thing that will occupy their minds is finding out whether they were right. Getting students to predict, therefore, gives a stronger motivation to proceed to the next step of the lesson. This is particularly useful in listening comprehension. There is all the difference in the world between listening to something to get some information and listening to something to see whether you were right.

4 **Enjoyment.** Enjoyment isn't just an added extra, an unnecessary frill. It is the simplest of all ways of engaging the learner's mind. The most relevant materials, the most academically respectable theories are as nothing compared to the rich learning environment of an enjoyable experience. This is an aspect of pedagogy that is taken for granted with children, but is too often forgotten with adults. It doesn't matter how relevant a lesson may appear to be; if it bores the learners, it is a bad lesson.

5 **An integrated methodology.** Using a range of skills greatly increases the range of activities possible in the classroom. This makes it easier to achieve a high degree of recycling and reinforcement, while maintaining the learners' interest.

6 **Coherence.** It should be clear where a lesson is going. Each stage should build on previous stages and lead naturally into the following stages.

7 **Preparation.** Lesson preparation is normally interpreted as the teacher planning the stages of the lesson. But as well as preparing the teacher to teach, we should also be preparing the learners to learn. It will be noticeable in the model lessons that the preparation for an activity forms the greater part of the lesson. This is a matter of building up a context of knowledge around the materials and so preparing the learners' minds to learn.

8 **Involvement.** Learners need to be involved both cognitively and emotionally in the lesson. We have set out already some of the ways in which learners can be involved (prediction, variety etc.). One of the simplest ways is asking questions. Don't tell learners things they know already; use guiding questions to get them to tell you and the rest of the class. But there are two words of warning here:
   a) Don't ask questions that are difficult to answer, such as defining questions, for example, 'What is an experiment?'
   b) Wait for the answer. Learners should feel that their contribution to the lesson is of value. This is part of their emotional involvement.

9 **Creativity.** Language is dynamic. Lessons should reflect this. Activities

should therefore allow for different possible answers, different levels of response. Different does not mean wrong. (Stevick, 1982)

10 **Atmosphere.** For all that we might try to analyse and systematise teaching, we must still recognise that effective learning depends heavily on intangible factors, such as the relationship between teacher and student. The cultivation of a cooperative social climate within the classroom is very important. This is particularly the case for ESP, where there are often other factors militating against a good atmosphere – a teacher, who is unsure of the materials or who actively dislikes the subject area; learners who resent the time they have to devote to English etc.

Conclusion

It is impossible to deal adequately with methodology in a book. It has to be experienced in the classroom. We have tried in this chapter to show some techniques which can help to make the ESP classroom a livelier, more enjoyable and thus more effective environment for both learner and teacher. Before we conclude the chapter, however, it is necessary to repeat two very important points.

a) There is nothing specific about ESP methodology. The principles which underlie good ESP methodology are the same as those that underlie sound ELT methodology in general. Similarly, at the level of techniques the ESP teacher can learn a lot from General English practice. The teacher who has come to ESP from General English need not think that a whole new methodology must be learnt. The classroom skills and techniques acquired in General English teaching can be usefully employed in the ESP classroom.

b) What happens in the classroom is not just an afterthought to be grafted on to ready-made materials and syllabuses. The activities in the classroom should feed back to all the other stages in the course design. As we saw with the Blood Cell in chapter 9, if you can create a useful activity by changing a text, change it. It is the activity that counts: 'I do and I understand.'

Tasks

1 Look at the *analysis* section (p. 139). Find specific examples of the points made in the model lessons.

2 A good lesson will try to make use of all the resources in the classroom, particularly those resources that learners bring to the lesson. What resources do the model lessons exploit?

3 What knowledge is required of learners and teachers in these lessons (specialist knowledge, general knowledge, linguistic knowledge, knowledge of communication)?

4 Take a sample of ESP materials that you use. Adapt them to incorporate 'gaps'.

12 Evaluation

Ah, but a man's reach should exceed his grasp,
Or what's a heaven for?

(Robert Browning: 'Andrea del Sarto')

We noted in the first section of this book that ESP had developed in response to certain pressures. Developments in the theoretical bases of language teaching were indicating a need to pay more attention to the individual learner, and at the same time the worlds of commerce and technology were producing a host of people with specific language learning needs. A demand was generated as a result for courses which would equip particular learners with the necessary skills to carry out particular tasks in English (or any other specified language). These same pressures have generated an equally strong need for a more open and coherent approach to evaluation. Any language teaching course has certain evaluation requirements, but in ESP these requirements are brought sharply into focus by the fact that the ESP course normally has specified objectives. ESP is accountable teaching. ESP learners and sponsors are investors in the ESP course and they want to see a return on their investment of time and/or money. The managers of the ESP course are accountable to these investors. This accountability has produced a demand for more and better evaluation procedures. Two levels of evaluation have thus been brought into prominence:

A *Learner assessment.* As with any language course there is a need to assess student performance at strategic points in the course, for example, at the beginning and at the end. But this assessment takes on a greater importance in ESP, because ESP is concerned with the ability to perform particular communicative tasks. The facility to assess proficiency is, therefore, central to the whole concept of ESP. The results of this kind of evaluation, for example, enable sponsors, teachers and learners to decide whether and how much language tuition is required.

B *Course evaluation.* A second important form of evaluation is the evaluation of the ESP course itself. This kind of evaluation helps to assess whether the course objectives are being met – whether the course, in other words, is doing what it was designed to do. (This type of evaluation should be a feature of any kind of ELT course. Unfortunately, it is rarely attempted in the General English context, even though there are sound educational reasons for doing so.)

These two forms of evaluation are not always distinct. Evaluation of the learners reflects not just the learners' performance but to some extent the effectiveness or otherwise of the course too. An ESP course is, after all, supposed to be successful: it is set up in order to enable particular learners to do particular things with language. If it consistently fails to meet this objective, then something must be wrong with the course design: the objectives may be too ambitious given the resources available; the analysis of the learners' initial competence may be wrong; the methodology may be inappropriate. Evaluation of the learners is unlikely to indicate exactly where a fault lies, but it will at least indicate the existence of a fault somewhere. More precise diagnostic evaluation can then be used to trace the fault.

In this sense, then, both course and learner evaluation have a similar function in providing feedback on the ESP course. However, each type of evaluation also has other purposes and procedures. Thus, while bearing in mind their similarity of role as feedback, we shall consider these two kinds of evaluation separately.

A Learner assessment

In spite of the importance, noted above, which ESP should logically give to assessment of student performance, there is a general lack of discussion or guidance on ESP testing. Munby (1978), for example, while laying down highly detailed procedures for the specification of learning objectives, makes no mention at all of how these objectives might be tested.

Alderson and Waters (1983) maintain that the lack of importance assigned to evaluation can be attributed to pervasive prejudices against testing among applied linguists and other language teaching practitioners. The result of this prejudice is to see assessment as a *post hoc* operation – a regrettable and dreary task to be tacked on to the end of the course design usually long after the syllabus, materials and methodology have been fixed. The net result is 'a paradoxical situation in which the need for better tests and evaluation procedures co-occurs alongside an almost universal lack of acceptable instruments' (ibid).

This lack, however, does not imply that there are no tests available in ESP. In fact Davies and West (1984) list 14 examinations in Specific Purpose English offered by British institutions. The London Chamber of Commerce and Industry, the Associated Examination Board (AEB) and Pitman Examinations Institute offer examinations in Secretarial and

Commercial English. Cambridge offers English for Business and English for Science. The City and Guilds of London Institute offers examinations in Technical English. AEB also offers an examination in English for Academic Purposes (TEEP), as does the British Council (ELTS). The English Language Teaching Development Unit (ELTDU) has produced a Scales of Attainment and Test Battery for Occupational English. There is, then, no shortage of available examinations in ESP. What is lacking is any sound theoretical or empirical basis for ESP testing. Far more research is needed before we will really know what the requirements of a good ESP test are. We shall return to this point below (p. 150).

In ESP there are three basic types of assessment:

1 Placement tests. These are used to 'place' learners in the ESP course most suited to their needs. The placement test normally comes at the beginning of the course.
2 Achievement tests. These test how well the learner is keeping up with the syllabus and can be administered any time through the course.
3 Proficiency tests. These assess whether or not the student can cope with the demands of a particular situation, for example, study at a university or reading technical manuals.

These different types of test do not necessarily vary in terms of content. They differ in terms of their initial function. But even here they need not be exclusive, since the same test may be used for more than one purpose. For example, all three types may be used as diagnostic tests, that is, tests to determine the areas of weakness a particular learner might have. This diagnostic evidence can then be used as a means of determining what and how much tuition the learner needs. The AEB's Test in English for Educational Purposes is a good example of a test with a dual function. It is used both to assess a student's ability to cope with a course of study (proficiency test) and to indicate what further help the learner might need (placement test).

1 Placement tests

The aim of the placement test is to determine the learners' state of knowledge before the ESP course begins. In so doing it should indicate firstly whether the learners need the course at all and secondly, should a need be indicated, what form the course should take. The placement test is, therefore, in the first instance a proficiency test. If a learner is already proficient in the skills required, no further tuition is required. In its second function, the placement test is diagnostic, indicating how far and in what ways the learner falls short of the proficiency level. In this respect the test has a formative value, in that the test results will be used in forming the nature and content of the ESP course that the learner will take. As already noted, the AEB's Test in English for

Educational Purposes can be used in this way for prospective students in higher education. ELTDU's Scales of Attainment provides a similar service for commercial and industrial use. The Scales specify the linguistic requirements of given tasks and the associated Test Battery determines what tasks an employee is currently able to do. Matching the results of the Test Battery to the Scales will provide a specification, which can provide the basis for future language training.

Doubts have been expressed about the ability to accurately diagnose learner needs through tests (Alderson and Hughes, 1981), but in the absence of any more accurate instruments, the course designer has little choice. What should be borne in mind is that any placement test can only be an approximate guide and should be treated with due caution. The good placement test should also reveal positive factors. It should show not just what the learner lacks, but also what potential for learning can be exploited in the ESP course.

2 Achievement tests

This kind of test is the least problematic, since it is usually internal to the course. It does not have to conform to external influences, but should rather reflect the nature and content of the course itself (Alderson and Hughes, 1981). The achievement test is, however, the kind of test the ESP teacher is most likely to have to construct. We will, therefore, give some basic guidance in this task (see e.g. Heaton, 1975 and Oller, 1979 for detailed guidance). In constructing a good ESP achievement test you should follow the same basic principles as you would for constructing any test. For example:

a) Test what you can reasonably assume the learners have learnt. This is not necessarily the same as what you have taught.

b) Your test should test what you actually want it to test. Don't, for example, make a test of reading ability dependent on the ability to write. A learner may well be able to read and understand something, but unable to put the ideas down in writing.

c) Avoid bias in the test. Don't, for example, write test items which demand specialist subject knowledge or cultural knowledge. This is a problem with any kind of language test, but it is probably more apparent in ESP tests, which may often involve the use of specialist content – technical, commercial, medical, and so on. The important point is that getting the correct answer should not depend on specialist subject knowledge *outside* the material used in the test.

Here is a sample test intended to assess mastery of the work done in the Blood Cell unit on page 110.

TEST

The diagram below shows the flow of coolant through a refrigeration system. Study the diagram and then write a description of how the coolant circulates through the system.

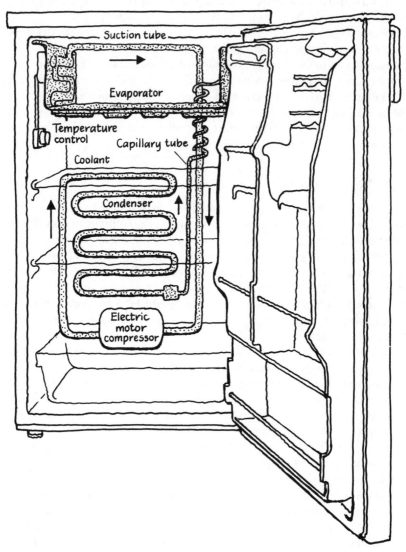

Figure 39: *A sample achievement test*

What features does this test have that make it a suitable means of evaluating the learners' understanding of the material?

a) It involves production as well as understanding. It, therefore, tests what the materials were teaching. A test which concentrated on, say, checking comprehension of a reading passage about how the refrigerator works would not test the ability to *produce* descriptions, which is one of the aims of the materials.

b) It is an integrated task rather than a set of discrete-point tests focussing on particular sub-skills, for example, 'linking clauses'. It is more economical to test the sub-skills by asking the students to combine them into a self-sufficient piece of discourse. An integrated test also tests the ability of the learners to use the sub-skills in a coherent piece of communication.

c) The content is of a similar nature to that of the unit: it is concerned with the movement of a fluid through an enclosed system. It should, therefore, indicate whether the learner is able to describe such systems.

d) The subject matter is probably already known to the learners. (In practice it would be wise to check this beforehand.) The subject knowledge should, therefore, neither obstruct nor give unfair advantage.

e) It does not require knowledge of subject-specific vocabulary, such as 'auricle' and 'ventricle'. The specific vocabulary of the refrigerator system is also given. The test, therefore, does not test subject-specific vocabulary, but rather the ability to exploit such vocabulary within a context of general vocabulary. The learners must extract the specific names from the diagram and use them in their description.

f) It tests written production. This might not be appropriate in every case. It would depend on how the unit had been taught. If the exercises in the materials had been done orally, then the test could be changed into an oral test as follows:

'Study the diagram. Then prepare and give an oral commentary on the flow of coolant through the system.'

3 Proficiency tests

In the introduction to their *Guide to English Language Examinations*, Davies and West (1984) identify the primary purpose of language testing in the eighties as 'proficiency testing designed to assess whether candidates will be able to perform the language tasks required of them'. Such tests, they say, are primarily criterion-referenced. In other words, the candidate's ability is assessed according to how far it matches certain criteria judged to be essential for proficiency in a particular task. With criterion-referencing, there is no *pass/fail* distinction, but rather a scale of degrees of proficiency in the task. An example of such a scale is that used for the British Council's ELTS test which is used to assess a candidate's ability to study at an English-medium institution of higher education:

Band Description
9 Expert User: fully operational command of the language; appropriate, accurate and fluent with complete understanding.
8 Very Good User: fully operational command of the language; occasional minor inaccuracies, inappropriacies or misunderstandings possible in unfamiliar situations.
7 Good User: operational command of the language; occasional inaccuracies, inappropriacies and misunderstandings in some situations.
6 Competent User: generally effective command of the language, although occasional misunderstanding and lack of fluency could interfere with communication.
5 Modest User: partial command of the language coping with overall meaning in most situations although some misunderstanding and lack of fluency could block communication.
4 Limited User: basic functional competence limited to familiar situations, but frequent problems in understanding and fluency can make communication a constant effort.
3 Extremely Limited User: below level of functional competence; although general meaning can be conveyed and understood in simple situations there are repeated breakdowns in communication.
2 Intermittent User: no real communication possible although single-word messages may be conveyed and understood.
1 Non-User: unable to use the language or does not provide relevant evidence of language competence for assessment.

Figure 40: *Proficiency scales used in ELTS test*

The move towards proficiency testing fits very neatly with the concept of ESP, which is crucially concerned with enabling learners to perform certain language tasks. Proficiency tests for specific purposes should, therefore, be able to give a reliable indication of whether a candidate is proficient enough to carry out the tasks that will be required. Such tests also have high face validity in that they look as if they are reliable indicators. Scientists might well question the results of a test which, for example, assessed their proficiency in writing reports on the basis of their ability to answer questions on a short story. But a test which asked for a report on a science lecture would seem to be a valid indicator of the required proficiency. Yet although specific language proficiency tests seem to be a logical extension of the ESP principle, they remain problematic. Why is this so?

a) As already noted, proficiency tests are primarily criterion-referenced. And therein lies the problem: what should the criteria be? Should they vary with different subject areas? What skills and knowledge enable someone to perform particular tasks? How specific are those skills and that knowledge to any particular task? In spite of all the recent developments in our knowledge of language use, we still have to admit that we do not really know what makes communicative performance possible. This argument might be countered by having real-life tasks as tests. However, this is rarely possible to set up in practice and so still leaves us with the problem of determining what features are crucial to the real-life performance.

b) How specific is specific? Can a test in Engineering, for example, be a valid indicator for all branches of Engineering – marine, electronic, civil, electrical, mechanical, aeronautical etc? Alderson and Hughes (1981) make this point in considering the British Council's ELTS test: 'which ELTS modular test, for example, out of the six presently available (Physical, Life, Social and Medical Sciences, Technology and General Academic) should be taken by a student of Urban and Regional Studies, whose course will include Law and Economics courses as well as courses in Technology?...What about the (frequent) cases of students who have a background in Physical Sciences, who are coming to the UK to do a (to them) novel course in Technology? Do they take the Physical Science test or the Technology test?'

Until we know more about what enables a language user to perform particular communicative tasks, we must view proficiency tests as only approximate guides.

Conclusion

In this section we have considered some of the mechanics of evaluating learner performance, and in particular we have outlined some of the problems associated with specific purpose testing. We should like, in conclusion, to consider the role that tests play within a learning-centred approach to ESP.

The value of tests depends primarily on how they are used. Teachers and learners need, first of all, a positive attitude to tests. Since tests are here to stay (at least until we can think of a better alternative), it is no good closing our eyes to them and hoping they will go away. Rather, tests should be recognised for the important role they play in the teaching-learning process, and every effort made – by teachers and learners – to get the most out of them. We need to see test results less as an end in themselves and more as the starting point for genuine negotiation and interaction between the teacher and the learners, and among the learners themselves. A grade, however good or bad, is in itself of little significance: its real meaning lies in understanding the reasons why it was given and what it tells the students about how they might improve their future work.

Evaluation can fulfil two functions – *assessment* and *feedback*. Assessment is a matter of measuring what the learners already know. But any assessment should also provide positive feedback to inform teachers and learners about what is still not known, thus providing important input to the content and methods of future work. Although used in the first instance to assess learner performance, the key to the development of a positive attitude to tests lies in recognising and capitalising on their feedback function, and playing down the obsessive or fearful attitudes engendered by viewing tests exclusively as determiners of grades. Given, also, the fact that most ESP learners are adults, there is no reason why the educational use of tests should not be taken a stage further, with learners becoming increasingly involved in providing feedback to themselves and their peers, and sharing in decisions about the most appropriate procedures for evaluating their progress. Such work can involve both useful realistic communication practice and deepen the learners' awareness of the learning process.

B Course evaluation

The ESP course, like any course, should regularly demonstrate that its continued existence in its present form is justified. Since the ESP course exists to satisfy a particular educational need, evaluation helps to show how well the course is actually fulfilling the need. A sponsor may also wish to be supplied with clear information about the suitability of the course and may well base decisions as to further investment and support on the results.

Thus evaluating an ESP course helps to establish whether it is meeting its aims. The information gathered forms the starting point for any necessary revisions of the course, and may also help to guide the design of other similar courses in your teaching institution or elsewhere. Course evaluation also plays a useful social role, by showing the various parties involved (teachers, learners, sponsors etc.) that their views are important. There are four main aspects of ESP course evaluation to be considered (Alderson and Waters, 1983):
a) What should be evaluated?
b) How can ESP courses be evaluated?
c) Who should be involved in the evaluation?
d) When (and how often) should evaluation take place?

a) *What should be evaluated?*

The short answer is: everything of significance. However, there are two important constraints:
i) Your ability to collect the information;
ii) Your ability to use the information once it has been collected. It will annoy everyone concerned if you collect all sorts of detailed evaluation information, possibly at considerable inconvenience, time and expense, and then do little or nothing with it. Next time round, your colleagues (and others) may not be so cooperative.

In a learning-centred approach to ESP, the overall aim of the ESP course is to meet two main needs of the learners: their needs as language *learners*, and their needs as language *users* (see chapter 6). It follows that the 'what' of ESP course evaluation is concerned with assessing the extent to which the course satisfies both kinds of needs. Thus, the enquiry should begin with questions such as:

Is the course fulfilling the learners' language *learning* needs?
Has the course fulfilled ⎱
Is the course fulfilling* ⎰ the learners' language *using* needs?

If the response to any of these questions is a 'yes', then congratulations are in order! However, assuming that you get only a qualified 'yes', (or even an outright 'no'!) in reply to one or more of them, the next question that needs to be asked is:

What areas of need are not being / have not been fulfilled?

Once we know what these areas are, we can turn our attention to identifying the source(s) of these problems. Now the relevant questions are:

Were the unfulfilled needs identified during the course design process? If not, why not?
How can the course design process be improved to avoid this problem in future?
How can the course be changed to take these needs into account?
If these needs *were* identified during the course design process, why are they not being / have they not been fulfilled? Is the fault in:
a) the syllabus(es);
b) the materials;
c) the teaching and learning techniques;
d) the testing procedures;
e) logistical/administrative arrangements;
f) the course evaluation system?

b) *How can ESP courses be evaluated?*

In theory, there are very many ways in which the ESP course can be evaluated, ranging from simulations to suggestion boxes. However, in practice, most ESP courses are evaluated using one or more of the following techniques:
– test results;
– questionnaires;

---

* The additional form of the question is for situations where exposure to the target situation occurs within the duration of the ESP course.

– discussions;
– interviews;
– informal means (e.g. unsolicited comments, 'casual' chats etc.).

Which techniques you use will depend on what suits your teaching situation best. It needs to be stressed that gathering the evaluation information is only the first stage in the process. The information must next be collated, and if it is extensive, summarised. After this, it needs to be discussed with all interested parties, and some conclusions drawn. Finally, it should be included in a detailed course evaluation report, as a basis for further discussions and decision-making. As with (a) above, nothing is more discouraging than if useful suggestions for change are consigned to the wastepaper bin through apathy or laziness on the part of teachers or course designers. Having reached your conclusions, use them!

c) *Who should be involved in the evaluation?*

The extent of involvement of any group will vary, but it is likely, in practice, that the bodies most closely concerned will be the ESP teaching institution, the ESP teachers, the learners and the course sponsors. (Former students can also provide useful information.) It is important to get a representative cross-section of views and to take them properly into account. Evaluation is concerned with people's perceptions of value and their views will, therefore, vary according to their own interests and concerns. With learners, in particular, it can be difficult to get feedback which is an expression of their real views. They may be reluctant to criticise authority, possibly thinking it might prejudice their assessment. They might simply be apathetic, feeling that any course revisions will not help them, but only future students. Orientation exercises (see Waters, 1985) can be used to get learners accustomed to expressing their views honestly and candidly, although it must be said that an open and trusting relationship between the teacher and the students is the best basis for promoting frank and useful feedback.

Who you ask and how you ask will affect what you find out. Thus, the methodology of course evaluation procedures, although coming midway in our list of points here, should actually be seen as a primary consideration, and care should always be taken, in any statement about evaluation findings, to make explicit how the information was obtained, that is, from whom, and by what means.

d) *When (and how often) should evaluation take place?*

There is an undoubted danger in doing course evaluation too frequently. Respondents have only so much time to give the right quantity and quality of information: the ESP teacher is limited in how quickly and insightfully he or she can process it and so on. However, the dangers in not doing course evaluation often enough are equal, or greater. Learners, sponsors and others will evaluate the course informally anyway. If there is no proper channel or forum for these views, there is a risk of misunderstanding, or at worst, hostility.

It is difficult to prescribe how often course evaluation should be done. All sensitive and responsive teaching will include this as a continuing feature anyway. So much will also depend on the characteristics of the individual teaching situation. However, in our experience, the most important times occur:

i)   in the first week of the course. The tone established here will probably have a greater overall effect on the success of the course than what occurs later, since initial impressions are very often more enduring than later ones.

ii) at regular intervals throughout the course, for example, every half term.

iii) at the end of the course.

iv) (if possible) after the course. This is potentially the most valuable, since the learners will be in a position to judge how well the course prepared them for the target situation they are now in.

Finally, a general word of caution. Evaluation can be time-consuming, complex and frustrating. Apart from the matters already discussed, other possible difficulties may arise. For example, problems identified might have no obvious solution, or only solutions that are too radical or expensive for everyone to accept. Feedback from one party may contradict feedback from another. In some parts of the world, willingness to evaluate in consultation with the learners might be taken as a sign of incompetence: 'It's the teachers' job to know these things – why should we do their job?' Alternatively, criticising a course might be seen as showing a lack of respect for authority. On the other hand, an evaluation session can easily degenerate into a forum for airing minor, personal grievances. Recognising that course evaluation is likely to bring with it disadvantages of this kind, as well as benefits, is probably half the battle. And, in overall terms, it is likely that a sound evaluation system will provide a deeper insight, from all sides, into the nature of the most effective learning experiences and processes that can be accommodated. As Brumfit (1983) says:

'One of the most useful roles of formal feedback sessions (is) to reveal to students the wide variety of their own demands and needs, so that they (become) increasingly aware of the need for a general syllabus which (can) be individualised within boundaries imposed by finance and time.'

Thus, in addition to its 'political' aspects, course evaluation, at its best, is an indispensable part of a learning-centred approach to ESP.

Conclusion

At the beginning of this chapter we identified two kinds of evaluation: evaluation of the student and evaluation of the course. We have outlined ways in which both kinds of evaluation can be carried out and we have described how each fits into a learning-centred approach. For student assessment, it means emphasising what tests can tell us about learning needs. In course evaluation we need to involve all those who share the learning process in making the ESP course as satisfying to the parties as possible. The origins of ESP lie in satisfying needs. Evaluation helps to assess how well the needs that have created the demand for a course are being served.

Tasks

1 Take one of the model lessons in chapter 11. Write a test to go with it. Explain what your test tests and how.

2 How does ESP testing differ from General English testing? What particular problems does the ESP tester face?

3 Look at the ELTS bands. What bands would you put your own learners in?

4 Evaluate your own ESP course. What would you evaluate? Who would you involve? What would you do with the information?

Section 4   *The role of the ESP teacher*

Give us the tools and we will finish the job.

(Winston Churchill)

Our explorations of the land of ESP are almost complete, and we come in this final section to consider the role of the ESP teacher, in particular, to consider in what ways the ESP teacher's lot differs from that of the General English teacher. We have stressed a number of times the need to see ESP within the context of language teaching in general and this applies as much to the role of the teacher as to materials and methodology. Nevertheless, there are important practical ways in which the work of the General English teacher and the ESP teacher differ. We shall conclude our journey by considering two of the most important differences, the one briefly and the other at greater length.

Firstly it will be clear from the preceding chapters that the ESP teacher's role is one of many parts. Indeed Swales (1985) prefers with some justification to use the term 'ESP practitioner' rather than 'ESP teacher' in order to reflect this scope. It is likely that in addition to the normal functions of a classroom teacher, the ESP teacher will have to deal with needs analysis, syllabus design, materials writing or adaptation and evaluation. We do not intend to go into this aspect in any further detail: the whole book is a testimony to the range of parts the ESP teacher is called upon to play. The second way in which ESP teaching differs from General English teaching is that the great majority of ESP teachers have not been trained as such. They need, therefore, to orientate themselves to a new environment for which they have generally been ill-prepared. This section will deal with this matter of orientation. The Appendix details sources of information to help the ESP teacher.

13 Orientation

> I have been a stranger in a strange land.
>
> (Exodus 2:22)

ESP teachers are all too often reluctant dwellers in a strange and uncharted land. In this chapter we shall consider this situation in greater detail, focussing on three problems which we have found consistently arise in discussions with teachers of ESP:
1 the lack of an ESP orthodoxy to provide a ready-made guide;
2 the new realms of knowledge the ESP teacher has to cope with;
3 the change in the status of English Language Teaching.
We shall consider each of these and offer some suggestions as to how a learning-centred approach can help.

1 The lack of an orthodoxy

In spite of its relatively brief existence, ESP has undergone a number of major shifts in orientation. These have come about largely because ESP has developed at a time when a fundamental revision of our view of language and learning has been taking place. Lacking a long tradition which might give some stability, ESP has frequently been a hotbed of conflict – the Wild West of ELT. New settlers in this land must often have found it difficult to find their bearings with no agreed maps to guide them. The question of authentic texts will illustrate the kind of problem that arises.

In the early stages of ESP there was no question of using authentic texts. Writers such as A. J. Herbert (1965) created their own texts to highlight language features much in the same way as was done in General English. This tradition was continued in the era of discourse analysis. Allen and Widdowson (1974), for example, defend the use of composed texts in order to 'avoid syntactic complexity' and to '"foreground" features of language which have particular communicative value'. Phillips and Shettlesworth (1978) on the other hand support the use of the authentic text 'as a repository of natural language use and ...as the stimulus for a variety of communication skills'. This matter of 'authenticity' is just one of the issues that continue to be debated amongst ESP practitioners. What is the newly arrived settler to make of this strange land of ESP under such circumstances? The answer is to return to basic principles and define exactly what is meant by 'using an authentic text'.

First of all, it is necessary to be clear what the term 'authentic' really means. It usually carries the sense of 'taken from the target situation and, therefore, not originally constructed for language teaching purposes'. In reality this is a contradiction of the term authentic. Authenticity is not a characteristic of a text in itself: it is a feature of a text in a particular context. A text alone has no value. A text is a message from a writer to an assumed reader. In writing the text the writer will make a judgement as to the knowledge the assumed reader will bring to the text and the use the reader will make of it. The text, therefore, only assumes a value in the context of that knowledge and that use. A text can only be truly authentic, in other words, in the context for which it was originally written. Since in ESP any text is automatically removed from its original context, there can be no such thing as an authentic text in ESP.

There is, therefore, no intrinsic merit in an 'authentic' text. What we have to do is once more to see the text as part of the teaching/learning process. The question should not be: 'Is this text "authentic"?' but 'What role do I want the text to play in the learning process?' We should be looking not for some abstract concept of 'authenticity', but rather the practical concept of 'fitness to the learning purpose'.

In this sense, it can easily be seen that different types of text will be required at different stages of a course, depending on what we want the text for, for example:

a) You want the learners to realise how much information they can get from a text by the application of certain strategies. In this case you might well want to use a target situation text to make the exercise more realistic.

b) You want to do a jigsaw reading task, such as in lesson 2 in chapter 11. If you insisted on using target situation texts here, you could be searching forever to find the appropriate ones. In this case, it is the activity that is of greatest importance and so the texts can be constructed to generate the best activity.

c) You want to illustrate a particular sentence pattern or discourse pattern. If you can find a target situation text that fits, use it. If not, it is no great problem. Your purpose is to make apparent an underlying structure. A target situation text might be rather confusing, because there are all sorts of other things in the text too (Allen and Widdowson, 1974). Here a simplified target text or a specially constructed one might be more useful.

d) You want to illustrate the importance of layout as a clue to reading comprehension. 'Authenticity', particularly of the visual appearance, is a *sine qua non* in this case.

e) You want to increase your learners' motivation by emphasising the real world application of the language. In this case, an 'authentic' text is preferable, or at least an 'authentic' appearance.

The importance of a text is not intrinsic to the text, but derives from the role the text has to play in the teaching/learning process. Ask yourself: 'What do I want the text to do?' On that basis the most appropriate type of text can be selected.

As the example of the use or non-use of authentic texts illustrates, ESP teachers will often have to orientate themselves to difficult problems with little or no guidance. There are no easy solutions to this situation, but some methods that might be useful are:

– surveys of the history and present state of ESP in your own or neighbouring countries;
– formation of groups of ESP teachers, perhaps allied to any existing national organisation for the promotion of ELT, to further the support and development of ESP;
– establishment of newsletters and other forms of publication, for exchanging information and views about ESP in your country;
– provision of pre- and in-service teacher training focussing on ESP issues. Such provision can take a variety of forms: workshops, seminars, short courses etc.

In short, ESP teachers cannot turn to linguistics and psychology in the hope of finding ready-made, straightforward answers to the problems that they will meet. Rather, they need to distil and synthesise, from the range of options available, those which best suit the particular circumstances. To do so requires an open mind, curiosity, and a degree of scepticism. ESP teachers need to arm themselves with a sound knowledge of both theoretical and practical developments in ELT in order to be able to make the range of decisions they are called upon to make. All ESP teachers are in effect pioneers who are helping to shape the world of ESP.

2 New realms of knowledge

As well as having to cope with the uncertain values of the strange land of ESP, ESP teachers may also have to struggle to master language and subject matter beyond the bounds of their previous experience. Teachers who have been trained for General English teaching or for the teaching of Literature may suddenly find themselves having to teach with texts whose content they know little or nothing about. Thus in addition to having to orientate themselves in a shifting world, ESP teachers may at the same time feel a sense of utter inadequacy at their ability to cope. This problem is best illustrated in the question of specialist knowledge and language. Put briefly, does the ESP teacher need to understand the subject matter of ESP materials?

Taken in isolation, the answer to this question must be 'yes'. Teachers of social or literary English would not enter the classroom understanding little about the content of the texts to be taught. So why should a different standard apply to the Science or Commerce text? But we need to look at this in a broader context, if we are going to be able to come up with a reasonable answer. We need to ask ourselves three questions:
a) Does the content of ESP materials need to be highly specialised?
b) Why do so many ESP teachers find it difficult to comprehend ESP subject matter?
c) What kind of knowledge is required of the ESP teacher?

a) *Does the content of ESP materials need to be highly specialised?*

As the work of the early pioneers in register analysis showed, there is little linguistic justification for having highly specialised texts. There is no clear relationship between sentence grammar and specialisation of knowledge. ·In specialised texts the discourse structure may be denser and more formalised, but not different in kind from that of less specialised material. There may well be a heavier load of specialist vocabulary, but this need not make it more difficult to understand (see below). Indeed it may make it easier, because many such terms are internationally used. In short, the linguistic knowledge needed to comprehend the specialist text is little different from that required to comprehend the general text. The difference in comprehension lies in the subject knowledge, not the language knowledge. As Hüllen (1981) says:

'...it is not the usage of technical terms *per se* which distinguishes language for special purposes from general language, but the factual knowledge necessary for understanding these words.'

The only real justification for having highly specialised texts is to achieve face validity. Learners may be more motivated by them, because they make the language seem more relevant. But learners can be very fickle. And if the use of such texts makes work in the classroom difficult, learners will soon lose their liking for such texts.

The real answer to this question lies in looking at the teaching of ESP in terms of a whole teaching/learning process. Any factor within that process must be evaluated on the basis of how it relates to the other factors and thus affects the entire process. Texts, in other words, should not be selected as texts, but as elements in a learning process. If the texts cannot be handled effectively by the teacher, it is not enough to simply expect the teacher to cope as well as possible. A reasonable solution should be negotiated.

We might compare this situation to cooking. Good ingredients are important for a successful meal. But they will not of themselves produce success. If the cook does not know how to exploit the ingredients well, or if the necessary equipment is lacking, or if the diners do not like that kind of cuisine, then the value of the ingredients will be little appreciated. Negotiation is needed: the competence of the cook, the ingredients and the tastes (and dietary needs) of the diners must all be taken into account. This, of course, does not preclude the possibility of retraining the cook or re-educating the palates of the diners.

So it is with ESP, materials must take proper account of the knowledge and competence of the teacher and negotiate a workable relationship. The starting point for such negotiation is the teacher's current state of knowledge. If teachers are unable to operate highly specialised texts effectively they should not be used. The teachers' competence is an essential ingredient in the teaching-learning process and must, therefore, be able to influence such matters as the choice of texts. In this regard it is fortunate that many ESP teachers are also course designers and materials writers. In contrast to their General English colleagues they do have the power to influence syllabuses and materials in order to accommodate their own capacities.

b) *Why do so many ESP teachers find it difficult to comprehend ESP subject matter?*

This problem arises from four causes:

i)   There is a tradition in education of separating the Humanities and the Sciences. Languages have usually been allocated to the Humanities camp. The result has been that English teachers often receive little or no education in the Sciences.

ii) Many ESP teachers are reluctant settlers in the new territory. They would prefer to be teaching Literature and Social English in the comfortable environs of ELT, but have been obliged by economic pressure to emigrate. This does not engender a great desire to learn about the new area.

iii) Considering the scale of the ESP revolution it must be admitted that little effort has been made to retrain teachers or to at least allay their fears. Jack Ewer's retraining programme in Chile is a notable exception (see Swales, 1985).

iv) The general attitude in ESP seems to be to expect teachers to conform to the requirements of the target situation. As noted above, this kind of one-way accommodation seems to us unreasonable.

The net result has been to produce a cadre of teachers, many of whom feel alienated by the subject matter they are expected to teach. Science and Technology, in particular, are seen as dull, boring, complicated, incomprehensible, confusing. This can only have a negative effect on teaching. It is, therefore, essential that any approach to ESP teacher training should try to dispel the fears and hostility that many teachers have towards ESP subject matter. They should be shown that specialist subject areas are not difficult to understand and can be interesting. Most important of all, they should be helped to realise that they already have much of the knowledge needed to understand the subject matter.

c) *What kind of knowledge is required of the ESP teacher?*

ESP teachers do not need to learn specialist subject knowledge. They require three things only:
i)   a positive attitude towards the ESP content;
ii)   a knowledge of the fundamental principles of the subject area;
iii) an awareness of how much they probably already know.
This can be summed up as 'the ability to ask intelligent questions'. When confronted with a machine, for example, the teacher should not necessarily know how it works, but should be able to ask:

What is the machine used for?
What's this part called?
Why does it do that?
Why doesn't it do that?
etc.

In other words, the ESP teacher should not become a teacher of the subject matter, but rather an interested student of the subject matter.

One final point to note is that, as with learner needs, teacher knowledge is not a static commodity. Many ESP teachers are surprised at how much knowledge of the subject matter they 'pick up' by teaching the materials or talking to students.

To sum up, if there is to be meaningful communication in the classroom, it is essential that there is a common fund of knowledge and interest between teacher and learner. This implies inevitably that the ESP teacher must know something about the subject matter of the ESP materials. However, in a learning-centred approach, this is not seen as a one-way movement, with the teacher having to learn highly specialised subject matter. Instead it should involve negotiation, where text subject matter takes account of the teacher's existing knowledge and at the same time efforts are made to help the teacher to acquire some basic knowledge about the subject. Of greatest importance is the need to dispel the mystique of specialist knowledge and build up the ESP teacher's confidence in coming to terms with it.

3 Change in the status of English teaching

One of the most important features of ESP in relation to General English is that the status of English changes from being a subject in its own right to a service industry for other specialisms. In many cases this leads to a lowering of status for the teacher, or at least this seems to be the ESP teachers' view. Johns (1981), for example, lists five problems that EAP teachers complain of: low priority in timetabling; lack of personal/professional contact with subject teachers; lower status/grade than subject teachers; isolation from other teachers of English doing similar work; lack of respect from students. These all seem to reflect either a lowering of status or at least a general feeling of inferiority on the part of ESP teachers. This is, however, not a universal phenomenon. In some situations ESP teachers enjoy high status. But, whatever the effect on the teachers' status, the result of a move to ESP is always to make the ESP teacher more accountable to others. As a result, in addition to the roles that we have already outlined – materials writer, syllabus designer, analyst etc. – the ESP practitioner frequently has to be a negotiator, too.

ESP teachers might, for example, find themselves having to work in close cooperation with sponsors or subject specialists who are responsible for the learners' work or study experience outside the ESP classroom. This is not always an easy relationship: suspicion of motives is common. The effectiveness of the relationship depends greatly on how it is handled by both parties, but, since it is usually the ESP teachers who have enlisted the help of the subject specialist, it is their main responsibility to ensure that potential problems are anticipated and avoided, and that a harmonious working arrangement is created. One of the keys to success in this area is for ESP teachers to establish clear guidelines about their and the specialist's separate and joint roles and responsibilities. Choice of the specialist counterpart also needs to be made carefully: the most available or 'knowledgeable' specialist may not be so useful as the one who has the best understanding of and greatest sympathy for ESP. Most important of all is that such cooperation should be a two-way process: the subject specialist can help the ESP teacher in learning more about the learners' target situation. At the same time the ESP teacher can make the subject specialist more aware of the language problems learners (and ESP teachers) face. More detailed treatment of this topic – often referred to as 'team teaching' – can be found in ELT Documents 106 and 112, and in Coleman (1983).

The ESP teacher may also have to negotiate in a more physical sense. Cramped classrooms, often in inconvenient locations, badly ventilated or heated, with a great deal of outside noise, are only too common. Equally, the teaching may take place in workshops or on the factory 'shop floor' (as in, e.g. EOP), or on the premises of businesses and other concerns, often without such basic classroom 'apparatus' as a blackboard. The role ESP teachers are called on to play here is obviously one of adaptability and flexibility. They need to be prepared to accept such conditions as to some extent inevitable, to strive to improvise while also patiently campaigning for improvements with the sponsors.

The most important way in which the ESP teacher becomes a negotiator is with regard to the learners, themselves. In contrast to the General English teacher, the ESP teacher is faced by a group of learners with certain expectations as to the nature, content and achievements of the course. We can see the effects of this most clearly if we consider the problem of having learners of several different subject specialisms in the same ESP class. It would seem something of a contradiction to try and teach ESP to Biologists, Engineers, Medical students and Architects in the same class. Yet this is quite frequently the situation that the ESP teacher is in. What can be done to give all the students what they need and want? In practical terms, how can you deal with apparently specific needs without using subject-specific materials? How can you negotiate a reasonable compromise, satisfactory to both teacher and learner?

Partly, of course, the problem is of our own making: relevance has been the great battle cry of ESP. As a result, an expectation has been built up in the learners that they will get the English for their own specific needs. But since a large number of teachers have to live with the problem, we need a more constructive answer than this. Let us look briefly at the justification for having subject-specific ESP materials.

In terms of language content, there is little reason why, say, a Biology text should be more useful to a Biologist than, say, a Physics text. There is no grammatical structure, function or discourse structure that can be identified specifically with Biology or any particular subject. Such things are the product of the communicative situation (lecture, conversation, experiment, instructions etc.) and the level (engineer, technician, manager, mechanic, university etc.). There are only two ways in which the subject has any kind of influence on the language content:

a) Vocabulary. But even here the differences are far less significant than might be expected. We can distinguish four types of vocabulary:
   −structural: e.g. are, this, only, however;
   −general: e.g. table, run, dog, road, weather, cause;
   −sub-technical: e.g. engine, spring, valve, acid, budget;
   −technical: auricle, schistosome, fissure, electrophoresis.
   It is only the last category that will show any significant variation

with subject. But the variation is small. Inman (1978), for example, found that in an extensive corpus of scientific and technical writing, technical vocabulary accounted for only 9 % of the total range of lexis. Furthermore, this technical vocabulary was used far less frequently than the non-technical. These technical terms are also likely to pose the least problems for learners: they are often internationally used or can be worked out from a knowledge of the subject matter and common word roots.

b) Certain subject areas show a higher proportion of particular grammatical or structural forms. For example, a register analysis of Scientific and Technological subjects will show a high percentage of passives and nominal/adjectival compounds (e.g. a 40 track disk drive); reports on experiments are very common in Chemistry, and so on. But these factors are of very limited value. Although the passive, is common in EST, the learner still needs both the active and the passive, and the fact that a form is more common does not make it any more difficult to learn. Nominal compounds are found everywhere in English, not just in Science and Technology (e.g. a coffee cup), and the rules for their creation and use do not vary with subject.

Thus, in terms of language content there is little justification for a subject-specific approach to ESP. The justification becomes even less significant when we take into account underlying skills and strategies. These certainly do not vary with the subject area.

But it is one thing for the ESP teacher to know that language needs vary little with subject; it is quite another to convince the learners that this is so. The reasons for having a subject-specific approach rest almost entirely on two affective factors generated by the learners themselves:

a) Face validity. Subject-specific materials look relevant.

b) Familiarity. If learners have got used to working with a particular kind of text in the ESP classroom they will be less apprehensive about tackling it in the target situation.

These factors should not be discounted. They are very important to the learners. But, having analysed the reason why learners often demand subject-specific texts, we can try to work out a strategy for dealing with the problem.

a) The first step is to try and establish groupings along broad subject lines: commerce and economics, physical sciences, medical and biological sciences etc. This should be within the reach of almost all institutions.

b) Avoid highly specific materials and try to give everyone's specialism some chance. In this way you may not please everyone all the time, but at least you won't displease anyone all the time.

c) Look for topics which give access to a number of different specialist areas. Take pumps as a simple example: pumps are found in the body (the heart), in houses (central heating systems), in engines (petrol pumps), in hospitals (peristaltic pumps in heart-lung machines) etc. Using topics like this, learners can apply the ideas and language of a core text to their own specialist field.

d) Make learners aware of the lack of specificity of their needs. You will not achieve this by simply telling them that they do not need subject-specific materials. Get them to discover it for themselves by doing their own language analysis. Find texts from different specialisms and get the learners to analyse the language to try and find out what makes one subject text different from another. In this way they should be able to see for themselves that the language is not significantly different. You can try a similar technique for skills/strategies. These activities will also incidentally provide some valuable language work.

e) If people are having fun, they are far less likely to complain. Making the methodology more interactive and enjoyable can be a valuable weapon in countering demands for subject-specific ESP.

In conclusion, then, there is little justification for having very specific materials. But learners will still demand them. Coping with this situation will be greatly eased by first of all trying to understand why learners demand such materials, then trying to negotiate a compromise: making learners more aware of their real needs and using an enjoyable methodology to divert attention from areas of possible conflict.

To return to the original point, the examples given illustrate the extra dimension that results from the change in the status of English when we move from the General English to the ESP situation. The teacher becomes accountable to other parties – sponsors, subject specialists, learners – and as such takes on the additional role of negotiator.

Conclusion

We have dealt in this final chapter with some of the features that distinguish the role of the ESP teacher from that of the General English teacher. We have shown with examples how in a learning-centred approach it is important to balance all the factors involved in the teaching-learning process. In this way the difficulties that many ESP teachers encounter can be reduced. At the same time we hope you will be encouraged to realise both what the land of ESP has to offer you and what knowledge and potential you bring with you to expand and develop this brave new world.

Finally, we should like to present a simple analogy to sum up the approach we have presented in this book.

There are three sports coaches, coaching a mixed team of athletes.

The first coach does a rigorous analysis of the abilities his players need. He analyses the anatomical structure of the perfect athlete and works out weight-training exercises for building up each important muscle.

The second coach decides that this is not the best approach. Rather than big powerful muscles, he feels that the players need to develop their skills in using the muscles. He creates a programme of endurance courses. He also thinks his players would work better if they knew why the different muscles acted as they did and how the body operates as a machine. So he builds work on anatomy and diet into his course.

The third coach decides that both these approaches have some good features but notices that the athletes don't like them very much. They are all keen to make the first team, but even so they often don't turn up to training sessions. He asks them what the problem is and what they would prefer to do. They say that the exercises and obstacle courses are very thorough and the information about diets is very relevant but it's all rather boring and repetitive. They would rather play some sort of game. The third coach then does another analysis. He works out what muscles and skills the players would use in a game of football or basketball and other activities. He then matches this analysis to the one done by the other coaches. He finds that there is a large degree of similarity. So he designs a programme of activities: football, basketball and other team games. While the players are doing these activities, he watches them. Every now and then, he stops the activities and teaches them a new technique or tells them something about why their bodies act as they do, or he might give some advice on diet or exercises to improve a particular skill.

We can compare these three coaches to the three approaches to ESP we have referred to in this book: a language-centred approach, a skills-centred approach and a learning-centred approach, respectively. In conclusion, we leave it to you to decide which coach and which approach will be the most successful.

Tasks

1 What roles are you called on to play as an ESP teacher? What additional roles might other ESP teachers have to play?

2 What can the ESP teacher do to improve his or her knowledge of specialist subjects?

3 Look at the four types of vocabulary given on page 165. Find a text from your learners' target situation and categorise the vocabulary in the same way. Compare your results to Inman's.

4 How far would you agree with Johns' five complaints (p. 164)? Make your own list.

5 Why do you think ESP teachers generally have, or regard themselves as having a lower status?

6 'If people are having fun, they are far less likely to complain. Making the methodology more interactive and enjoyable can be a valuable weapon in countering demands for subject-specific ESP.' How far would you agree with this?

Appendix: resources

1 Books

At the current time there is a general lack of books on ESP. This is changing and the next few years are likely to see more works published on the subject. Most of the resources of information available are, therefore, in the form of journals or collections of articles.

a) Of the few books currently available *ESP in Perspective – A Practical Guide* by Jo McDonough (Collins, 1984) gives a good general survey of the field.

b) Another recent book is *English for specific purposes* by Chris Kennedy and Rod Bolitho (Macmillan, 1984). This book gives a generally language-centred view of ESP.

c) Although not limited to ESP, Henry Widdowson's *Teaching Language as Communication* (OUP, 1978) is a very useful introduction to the nature of language as communication and approaches to treatment of the four skills. Of great value to practitioners of EST in particular, but also to anyone involved in any area of ESP, are Sections One, Two and Three of the same author's *Explorations in Applied Linguistics* (OUP, 1979). Many other parts of this book are also highly recommended e.g. chapters 12, 13, 14, 19 and 20. Widdowson's more recent *Learning Purpose and Language Use* (OUP, 1983) provides a theoretical framework for ESP, and explores some of its practical implications – another 'must' for the ESP devotee!

d) The discourse analysis approach to ESP is fully explained in *English for Science and Technology: A discourse approach* by Louis Trimble (CUP, 1985).

2 Surveys and collections of papers

a) The best general survey of the field is probably Pauline Robinson's *ESP* (*English for Specific Purposes*) (Pergamon, 1980). Although needing updating, it presents a balanced, comprehensive overview, and contains a very useful, extensive bibliography.

b) A number of issues of *ELT Documents* (Pergamon, formerly published by the British Council) provide a perspective on a wide spectrum of ESP work. Of particular interest are:

Nos. *101: English for Specific Purposes* (1978)
106: Team Teaching in ESP (1980)
107: The University of Malaya ESP Project (1980)
112: The ESP Teacher: Role, Development and Prospects (1981)

116: *Language Teaching Projects for the Third World* (1983)
117: *Common Ground: Shared Interests in ESP and Communication Studies* (1984)
ELT Documents Special Issues and Occasional Papers: Projects in Materials Design (1980).
An article, by Gerry Abbott, in another volume of the series (*103*: *Individualisation in Language Learning*), is also worth consulting as background reading, as is Chris Kennedy's response to Abbott's article in *ELT Documents 106*.
A volume of ELT Documents on Materials Evaluation is forthcoming.

c) From a standpoint which attempts to thoroughly address both theoretical and practical issues, we recommend *English for Specific Purposes* (Longman, 1978) edited by R. Mackay and A. J. Mountford. The book adopts a case-study approach. However, it should be noted that nearly all the cases in question are of the EAP variety, and most of them are concerned with the design of ESP courses for overseas students in the UK setting. Nevertheless, other chapters are relevant to ESP as a whole, and the chapters on textbook design (by Swales, Allen and Widdowson, and Bates) are well worth reading.

d) Volumes 1–4 of *Practical Papers in English Language Education* (Institute for English Language Education, 1978–1982) contain a number of larger papers on ESP, in which there are very full accounts of the thinking behind a number of ESP projects, and copious illustration of ideas in the form of materials, course design, and so on. Volume 5, entitled *Lancaster Practical Papers in English Language Education*: Issues in ESP (Pergamon, 1983) is devoted entirely to ESP.

e) *Episodes in ESP* (Pergamon, 1985), edited by John Swales, is a collection of seminal articles on ESP, from the last 20 years or so, with a commentary on each one by the editor. As such, it makes a very handy reference work, especially since some of the writings it contains are difficult to obtain any other way. This book provides a much needed historical perspective on the development of ESP. Swales states in the introduction to *Episodes in ESP* that he hopes to produce a follow-up book, which will be a comprehensive bibliography of ESP. We all hope it will not be long in coming.

f) A more specialised collection co-edited by Swales is *ESP in the Arab World*, edited by John Swales and Hassan Mustafa (Language Studies Unit, University of Aston, 1984).

g) The American tradition in ESP is well documented in *English for Academic and Technical Purposes* edited by Larry Selinker, Elaine Tarone and Victor Hanzeli (Newbury House, 1981).

3 Journals and papers

Numerous journals exist in the world of ESP, too many to mention here. We have selected those which have had the most consistent publishing record, in the hope that they will continue to be available.

a) A very useful survey article by Bernard Coffey, 'ESP-English for Specific Purposes', appeared in *Language Teaching* Vol. 17, No. 1 (CUP, 1984).

b) An earlier article in the same journal (then known as *Language Teaching & Linguistics: Abstracts*) by Peter Strevens, 'Special purpose language learning: a perspective' was published in Vol. 10, No. 3, 1977.

c) Pergamon publish *The ESP Journal* twice a year.

d) Until early 1985 *English for Specific Purposes*, a newsletter, was published monthly by the English Language Institute, Oregon State University, Corvallis, Oregon 97331, USA. Publication ceased in 1985. It remains to be seen whether it will be revived either at Corvallis or elsewhere.

e) *Espmena Bulletin*, recently resuscitated after something of a relapse appears once or twice a year: subscription information from the Editor, English Language Servicing Unit, Faculty of Arts, University of Khartoum, PO Box 321, Khartoum, The Sudan. Collected volumes of *Espmena* have recently become available.

f) *TEAM* the journal of the ELI at the College of Petroleum and Minerals at Dhahran, Saudi Arabia, is published three times a year, and is available free of charge.

g) The Brazilian National ESP Project puts out a useful journal called *The ESPecialist* and also occasional *Working Papers*. These give a generally skills-centred view of ESP. More information can be obtained from: Departamento de Ingles, PUC, Rua Monte Alegre, 984, 05014-Sao Paulo-SP, Brazil.

4 Information and courses

a) The ELI at Corvallis (see *Journals* above) houses the EST Clearinghouse. This comprises a collection of papers etc. At the present time it is not clear what will happen to the collection.

b) Collections of articles on ESP exist at the Institute for English Language Education, University of Lancaster, Lancaster, England and at the Language Studies Unit of the Department of Modern Languages, at the University of Aston, Birmingham, England.

c) A number of ESP teacher training courses exist at centres such as the Institute for English Language Education (University of Lancaster), Essex University, Aston & Birmingham Universities, and so on. The British Council's *TEFL/TESL: Academic Courses in the United Kingdom* (published annually) is a comprehensive guide to these and other courses available in the UK.

d) Finally, conferences can be another useful source of information and ideas. All the major international ones (e.g. IATEFL, TESOL, RELC) include ESP-oriented presentations and get-togethers. A European Symposium on LSP (Language for Specific Purposes) is held annually. Watch out for regional conferences occurring in your area!

5   Non-ELT sources

It is a good idea for all ESP teachers to try and develop their knowledge of the subject specialisms of their learners. You can learn a lot from the subject specialists and from the students themselves. However, often the most useful sources are books intended for the non-specialist, particularly ones written for children. These are useful, because they explain a lot of the background knowledge that subject specialists take for granted. There is a huge range of books available. Most publishers have some such books. We list only a few here:

For children

a) How it Works: Series 654 (Ladybird Books Ltd). Titles include: *The Camera, The Rocket, The Computer.*
b) Junior Science: Series 621 (Ladybird Books Ltd). Titles include: *Magnets, bulbs and batteries; Levers, pulleys and engines.*
c) Young Scientist Books (Usborne).
d) Visual Books (Macdonald). Titles include: *Aircraft, The Weather, Money*
e) Insiders (Macdonald). Titles include; *Hospital, Oil Rig, Airport, TV Studio.*

For adult non-specialists

f) Made Simple Series (W. H. Allen). Titles include: *Applied Economics; Chemistry; Office Practice; Statistics; Electronics.*
g) Basic Guide to ... (Readers Digest). Titles include; *Practical Electrics; Home Plumbing; Looking after your car; Working in Wood; Home Decorating.*

These books and others like them can also be very useful sources of ideas for materials.

Bibliography

Adamson, D. and Bates, M., *Nucleus: Biology*, Longman, 1976

Alderson, J. C., 'A Process Approach to Reading at the University of Mexico' in *ELT Documents Special Issues and Occasional Papers: Projects in Materials Design*, British Council, 1980

Alderson, J. C. and Hughes, A. (eds.), *ELT Documents 111: Issues in Language Testing*, British Council, 1981

Alderson, J. C. and Waters, A., 'A course in testing and evaluation for ESP teachers' in *Lancaster Practical Papers in English Language Education* Vol. 5, Pergamon, 1983

Alderson, J. C. and Urquhart, A. H. (eds.), *Reading in a Foreign Language*, Longman, 1984

Alderson, J. C. (ed.), *Lancaster Practical Papers in English Language Education* Vol. 6: Evaluation, Pergamon, 1985

Allen, J. P. B. and Widdowson, H. G., 'Grammar in Language Teaching' in Allen, J. P. B. and Corder, S. P. (eds.), *The Edinburgh Course in Applied Linguistics*, Volume two: Papers in Applied Linguistics, Oxford University Press, 1975

Allen, J. P. B. and Widdowson, H. G., 'Teaching the Communicative use of English' in *International Review of Applied Linguistics* XII, 1, 1974 (also in Swales (ed.), 1985)

Allwright, R. L., 'Perceiving and Pursuing Learners' Needs' in Geddes, M. and Sturtridge, G. (eds.), *Individualisation*, Modern English Publications, 1982

Allwright, R. L., (1978) 'Abdication and responsibility in language teaching' in *Studies in Second Language Acquisition*, Vol. 2/1, Indiana University Press

Allwright, R. L., 'The importance of interaction in classroom language learning' in *Applied Linguistics*, Vol. 5, No. 2, Summer 1984a

Allwright, R. L., 'Why don't learners learn what teachers teach? – the interaction hypothesis' in *Language Learning in Formal and Informal Contexts: Proceedings of a joint seminar of the Irish and British Associations of Applied Linguistics* held at Trinity College, Dublin 11–13 September 1984, edited by D. M. Singleton and D. G. Little, IRAAL, 1984b

Ausubel, D. P., Novak, J. D. and Hanesian, H., *Educational Psychology: a Cognitive View*, Holt, Rinehart and Winston, 1978

Barber, C. L. (1962), 'Some Measurable Characteristics of Modern Scientific Prose' in Swales (ed.), 1985

Bates, M. and Dudley-Evans, T., *Nucleus: General Science*, Longman, 1976

Bloomfield, L., *Language*, Allen and Unwin, 1935

Blundell, J. A. and Middlemiss, N. M. G., *English for the Business and Commercial World: Career Developments*, Oxford University Press, 1982

Breen, M. P. and Candlin, C. N., 'The essentials of a communicative curriculum in language teaching' in *Applied Linguistics* 1, 1980

Breen, M., 'Process syllabuses for the language classroom' in Brumfit, C. J. (ed.), *General English Syllabus Design, ELT Documents 118*, Pergamon, 1984

Brumfit, C., 'Teaching the "General" Student' in Johnson, K. and Morrow, K. (eds.), 1981

Brumfit, C., 'Creating coherence in ELT teacher training' in Jordan, R. R. (ed.), *Case Studies in ELT*, Collins 1983

Brumfit, C., *Communicative Methodology in Language Teaching*, Cambridge University Press, 1984

Candlin, C. N., Bruton, C. J. and Leather, J. H., 'Doctors in Casualty: Specialist course design from a data base' in *International Review of Applied Linguistics* 3, 1976

Candlin, C. N. and Breen, M., 'Evaluating and Designing Language Teaching Materials' in *Practical Papers in English Language Education* Vol. 2, Institute for English Language Education, University of Lancaster, 1980

Candlin, C. N., 'Syllabus Design as a Critical Process' in *Language Learning and Communication*, 3 (2), 1984

Carroll, B., *Testing Communicative Performance*, Pergamon, 1980

Chitravelu, N., 'English for Special Purposes Project' in *ELT Documents 107*, British Council, 1980

Chomsky, N., *Syntactic Structures*, Mouton, 1957

Chomsky, N., Review of B. F. Skinner, 'Verbal Behaviour', in *Language 35*, 26–58, reprinted in *The Structure of Language*, Fodor, J. A. and Katz, J. J. (eds.), Prentice Hall, 1964

Coffey, B., 'ESP – English for Specific Purposes' in *Language Teaching* Vol. 17, No. 1, January 1984, Cambridge University Press

Cohen, C. and Mannion, L., *Research Methods in Education*, Croom Helm, 1980

Coleman, H., 'English Teacher Should Attends' in *Lancaster Practical Papers in English Language Education* Vol. 5, Pergamon, 1983

Coleman, H., 'Talking shop: an overview of language work' in *International Journal of Social Language*, 51, 1985

Coles, M. C. and Lord, B. D., *The Savoy English Course for the Catering Industry*, Edward Arnold, 1973

Corder, S. P., *Introducing Applied Linguistics*, Penguin, 1973

Coulthard, M., *An Introduction to Discourse Analysis*, Longman, 1977

Cunningsworth, A., *Evaluating and Selecting EFL Materials*, Heinemann, 1984

Davies, A. and Currie, W., 'Aptitude & Nativeness', Paper prepared for the BAAL Conference, University of Essex, September 24th–26th 1971 (mimeo)

Davies, S. and West, R., *The Pitman Guide to English Language Examinations*, Pitman Publishing Ltd, 1984

Donovan, P., *Basic English for Science*, Oxford University Press, 1978

Dresner, J., Beck, K., Morgano, C. and Custer, L., *It's Up to You*, Longman Inc., 1980

Drobnic, K., 'Mistakes and Modification in Course Design: An EST Case History' in Todd Trimble, M., Trimble, L. and Drobnic, K. (eds.), *English for Specific Purposes: Science and Technology*, Corvallis, Oregon, Oregon State University Press, 1978

Eastwood, J., *English for Travel*, Oxford University Press, 1980

ELT Documents 107: University of Malaya ESP Project, British Council, 1980

Ewer, J. R. and Latorre, G., *A Course in Basic Scientific English*, Longman, 1969

Ewer, J. R. and Hughes-Davies, E. (1971), 'Further Notes on Developing an English Programme for Students of Science and Technology' in Swales (ed.), 1985

Ewer, J. R., 'Teacher training for Science and Technology: the specialized training of teachers and programme organizers' in Richards, J. (ed.), *Teaching English for Science and Technology*, Singapore University Press, 1976

Ferguson, N. and O'Reilly, M., *English for International Banking*, Evans, 1979

Fillmore, C. J., 'The case for case' in Bach and Harms (eds.), *Universals in Linguistic Theory*, Holt, Rinehart and Winston, 1968

Firth, J. R., *Papers in Linguistics: 1934–51*, Oxford University Press, 1957

Fitzpatrick, A. and Yates, C. St J., *Bid for Power*, BBC, 1983

Gardner, R. C. and Lambert, W. E., *Attitudes and Motivation in Second Language Learning*, Newbury House, 1972

Grellet, F., *Developing Reading Skills*, Cambridge University Press, 1981

Halliday, M. A. K., McIntosh, A. and Strevens, P., *The Linguistic Sciences and Language Teaching*, Longman, 1964

Heaton, B., *Writing English Language Tests*, Longman, 1975

Herbert, A. J., *The Structure of Technical English*, Longman, 1965

Herbolich, J. B. (1979), 'Box Kites' in *English for Specific Purposes*, Issue 29, ELI, Oregon State University Press, (reprinted in Swales (ed.), 1985)

Holmes, J., 'Needs Analysis: A rationale for course design' in *The ESPecialist*, No 3, July 1981

Holmes, J., 'Some Approaches to Course Design', *Working Paper* No. 7, Brazilian ESP Project, 1982

Howatt, A. P. R., *A History of English Language Teaching*, Oxford University Press, 1984

Hüllen, W., 'The teaching of English for specific purposes: a linguistic view' in Freudenstein, R., Beneke, J. and Pönisch, H. (eds.), *Language Incorporated: Teaching Foreign Languages in Industry*, Pergamon, 1981

Hutchinson, T., 'The Practical Demonstration' in *Practical Papers in English Language Education*, Vol. 1, Institute for English Language Education, University of Lancaster, 1978

Hutchinson, T., 'A Cognitive Approach to Grammar or The Sad Tale of Grammarella' in *World Language English* 4/1, Pergamon, 1984

Hutchinson, T., 'What's underneath? – An Interactive View of Materials Evaluation' in *ELT Documents 126: Textbook and Materials Evaluation*, Pergamon, 1987 (forthcoming)

Hutchinson, T., Waters, A. and Breen, M. P., 'An English Language Curriculum for Technical Students' in *Practical Papers in English Language Education*,

Vol. 2. Institute for English Language Education, University of Lancaster, 1979

Hutchinson, T. and Waters, A., 'Communication in the Technical Classroom: You just shove this little chappie in here like that' in *ELT Documents Special – Projects in Materials Design*, British Council, 1980

Hutchinson, T. and Waters, A., 'ESP at the Crossroads', 1980 in Swales (ed.), 1985

Hutchinson, T. and Waters, A., 'Performance and Competence in ESP' in *Applied Linguistics* II, 1, 1981

Hutchinson, T. and Waters, A., 'Creativity in ESP' in *Lancaster Practical Papers in English Language Education*, Vol. 5, Pergamon, 1983

Hutchinson, T. and Waters, A., 'How Communicative is ESP?' in *ELT Journal* 38, 2, April 1984

Hutchinson, T. and Waters, A., *Interface: English for Technical Communication*, Longman, 1984

Hymes, D., 'On Communicative Competence' in *Sociolinguistics*, Pride, J. B. and Holmes, J. (eds.), Penguin, 1972

Inman, M., 'Lexical analysis of scientific and technical prose' in Todd Trimble, M., Trimble, L. and Drobnic, K. (eds.), *English for Specific Purposes: Science and Technology*, Corvallis, Oregon, Oregon State University Press, 1978

Johns, T. F., 'Some problems of a worldwide profession' in *ELT Documents 112: The ESP Teacher: Role, Development and Prospects*, British Council, 1981

Johnson, K. and Morrow, K. (eds.), *Communication in the Classroom*, Longman, 1981

Kerr, R. and Smith, J., *Nucleus: Nursing Science*, Longman, 1978

Krashen, S. D., *Second Language Acquisition and Second Language Learning*, Pergamon, 1981

Krashen, S. D., *Principles and Practice in Second Language Acquisition*, Pergamon, 1982

Lackstrom, L., Selinker, L. and Trimble, L., 'Technical Rhetorical Principles and Grammatical Choice' in *TESOL Quarterly* 7/2, 1973

Littlewood, W., *Foreign and Second Language Learning*, Cambridge University Press, 1984

Maciel, A. M. B., Marmet, L. and Curcio Celia, M. H., 'Developing a System for Specifying Objectives' in *Working Paper* No. 11, Brazilian ESP Project, 1983

McDonough, S., *Psychology in Foreign Language Learning*, Allen and Unwin, 1981

Mackay, R., 'Identifying the Nature of the Learner's Needs' in Mackay, R. and Mountford, A. J. (eds.), *English for Specific Purposes*, Longman, 1978

Martin, E. (ed.), *The Penguin Book of the Physical World*, Penguin Books, 1976

Mead, R., 'Expectations and Sources of Motivation in EAP' in Kennedy, C. (ed.), *English Language Research Journal* No. 1, University of Birmingham, 1980

Morrow, K., 'Communicative Language Testing: Revolution or Evolution?' in Brumfit, C. J. and Johnson, K. (eds.), *The Communicative Approach to Language Teaching*, Oxford University Press, 1979

Bibliography

Munby, J., *Communicative Syllabus Design*, Cambridge University Press, 1978

Norman, S., *We Mean Business*, Longman, 1982

Nuttall, C., *Teaching Reading Skills in a Foreign Language*, Heinemann, 1982

Oller, J., *Language Tests at School*, Longman, 1979

Phillips, M. and Shettlesworth, C., 'How To Arm Your Students: A Consideration of Two Approaches to Providing Materials for ESP' in *ELT Documents 101: English for Specific Purposes*, British Council, 1978, (reprinted in Swales (ed.), 1985)

Prabhu, N. S., 'Procedural syllabuses', paper presented at SEAMEO Eighteenth Regional Seminar, 1983

Richterich, R. and Chancerel, J. L., *Identifying the Needs of Adults Learning a Foreign Language*, Pergamon, 1980

Richterich, R., 'A European Unit/Credit System for Modern Language Learning by Adults' in Van Ek, J. A. and Trim, J. L. M. (eds.), *Across the Threshold Level*, Pergamon, 1984

Robinson, P., *ESP (English for Specific Purposes)*, Pergamon, 1980

Rodgers, C., *Freedom to Learn*, Merrill, 1969

Sandler, P. L., *The Petroleum Programme: English for the Oil Industry*, BBC, 1980

Scott, M., 'Reading Comprehension in English for Academic Purposes (EAP)' in *The ESPecialist*, No. 3, July 1981

Selinker, L. and Trimble, L., 'Scientific and Technical Writing: the Choice of Tense' in *English Teaching Forum*, 14, 4, 1976

Smith, F., 'The Promise and Perils of Computerised Instruction', paper presented at Dartmouth House, London, June 1984

Stern, H. H., *Fundamental Concepts of Language Teaching*, Oxford University Press, 1983

Stevick, E., *Memory, Meaning and Method*, Newbury House, 1976

Stevick, E., *Teaching and Learning Languages*, Cambridge University Press, 1982

Stevick, E., 'Earl Stevick on humanism and harmony in language teaching' in *ELT Journal* Vol. 38, Number 2, April 1984

Strevens, P., *New Orientations in the Teaching of English*, Oxford University Press, 1977

Strevens, P., 'Language Learning and Language Teaching: towards an integrated model' lecture delivered to the LSA/TESOL Summer Institute, Georgetown University, 1985

Swales, J., *Writing Scientific English*, Nelson, 1971

Swales, J. (ed.), *Episodes in ESP*, Pergamon, 1985

Swan, M., 'A critical look at the Communicative Approach' (1) in *ELT Journal* 39/1, January 1985a

Swan, M., 'A critical look at the Communicative Approach' (2) in *ELT Journal* 39/2, April 1985b

Tarone, E., Dwyer, S., Gillette, S. and Icke, V., 'On the use of the passive in two Astrophysics journal papers' in *ESP Journal* 1, 2, 1981 (reprinted in Swales (ed.), 1985)

Trimble, L., *EST: A discourse approach*, Cambridge University Press, 1985

Van Ek, J. A., *Systems Development in Adult Language Learning: the Threshold Level*, Council of Europe, 1975

Van Ek, J. A. and Alexander, L. G., *Systems Development in Adult Language Learning: Waystage: an Intermediary Objective below Threshold Level*, Council of Europe, 1977

Wallace, M. J., *Study Skills in English*, Cambridge University Press, 1980

Waters, A., 'Involving ESP Learners in Course Evaluation' in *KMIT's EST Bulletin*, Vol. 3, No. 2, King Mongkut's Institute of Technology, Thailand, 1985

Widdowson, H. G., *Teaching Language as Communication*, Oxford University Press, 1978

Widdowson, H. G., *Explorations in Applied Linguistics*, Oxford University Press, 1979

Widdowson, H. G., (ed.), *Reading and Thinking in English*, Oxford University Press, 1979

Widdowson, H. G., 'English for Specific Purposes: Criteria for Course Design' in *English for Academic and Technical Purposes: Studies in Honor of Louis Trimble*, Selinker, L., Tarone, E. and Hanzel, V. (eds.), Newbury House, 1981

Wilkins, D. A., *Notional Syllabuses*, Oxford University Press, 1976

Acknowledgements

The authors and publishers are grateful for permission to reproduce copyright material:
p. 25 extract from *Nucleus: Nursing Science* by Rosalie Kerr and Jennifer Smith, p. 26 adapted extract from *A Course in Basic Scientific English* by J. R. Ewer and G. Latorre, p. 33 extract from *We Mean Business* by Susan Norman with Eleanor Melville, pp. 43–4 extract from *Nucleus: Biology* by Donald Adamson and Martin Bates, p. 86 extract from *Nucleus: General Science* by Martin Bates and Tony Dudley-Evans, pp. 110, 112, 114, 116, 130–1 extracts from *Interface: English for Technical Communication* by Tom Hutchinson and Alan Waters, Longman Group Ltd; p. 29 extracts from 'Performance and Competence in ESP' by Tom Hutchinson and Alan Waters in *Applied Linguistics* II.1, p. 32 extract from *English for Travel* by John Eastwood, extract from *Reading and Thinking in English: Exploring functions* Associate Editor Professor H. G. Widdowson, p. 40 extract from *Basic English for Science* by Peter Donovan, p. 87 extracts from *English for Secretaries, English for the Business and Commercial World: Career Developments* by J. A. Blundell and N. M. G. Middlemiss, *Reading and Thinking in English: Discovering discourse* Associate Editor Professor H. G. Widdowson, Oxford University Press; p. 35 extract from *English for International Banking* by Nicolas Ferguson and Maíre O'Reilly, Bell and Hyman; p. 41 extract from *Bid for Power: English for Commerce and Industry* Students' Book by A. Fitzpatrick and C. St J. Yates, p. 85 extract from *The Petroleum Programme: English for the oil industry* by P. L. Sandler, BBC English by Radio and Television; pp. 41 and 88 extracts from *It's Up to You* by Mission Language and Vocational School Inc. Copyright © 1980. Longman Inc. All Rights Reserved; pp. 44–6 extract from *ELT Documents 107*, The University of Malaya, English for Specific Purposes Project © the British Council 1980; p. 150 extract from ELTS test, The British Council; pp. 85–6 extract from *The Savoy English Course for the Catering Industry* by M. C. Coles and B. D. Lord, Edward Arnold Ltd; p. 91 skills-centred approach adapted from 'Needs Analysis: A rationale for course design' by John Homes in *The ESPecialist* No. 3, July 1981 © Projeto 'Ensino de Inglés Instrumental em Universidades Brasileiras' São Paulo, Brazil.

Index